RECORDING TECHNIQUES
for small studios

David Mellor

PC Publishing

PC Publishing
Export House
Tonbridge
Kent TN9 1SP
UK

tel 01732 770893
fax 01732 770268
email pcp@cix.compulink.co.uk
website http://www.pc-pubs.demon.co.uk

First published 1993
Reprinted 1997

ISBN 1 870775 29 5

British Library Cataloguing in Publication Data

Mellor, David
    Recording Techniques for Small Studios
    I. Title
    621.389

Printed and bound in Great Britain by Bell and Bain, Glasgow

Contents

Foreword

Never before in the history of sound recording has so much high level and high quality technology been available to the owner or user of a small recording studio.

Hard disk multi-track systems, synchronised digital multi-tracks and sampling devices that are now available would only have been a dream for most small studio operators a few years ago. Indeed many of these systems might not have been installed in the highest level of studio five years ago.

As I am writing this I am reflecting on the level of technology available when Gateway was first opened in 1975 and the fun and excitement we experienced in learning many new techniques and coping with the developments.

Those basic recording techniques are even more applicable with today's technology particularly as digital recording reveals any noise or distortion present in the process. It is very timely therefore that David Mellor's book on techniques for the small studio should be published at this time. This book complements the excellent reference book *Sound Recording Practice* published by the Association of Professional Recording Services and fills a much needed gap for a text book of this type.

For many years on all of the courses that Gateway has run, much emphasis has been placed on the dynamics of the recording session and the communication skills that are needed by producers and engineers to channel the creative process. When reading David's book I was very happy to find so many references to these often disregarded subjects. Recording is indeed a creative, communicative and cooperative process and not just a technological manipulation of electrical elements.
David Ward

David Ward is the Founder and Director of the Gateway School of Recording and Music Technology and owner of Gateway Studios who are in partnership with Kingston University.

The art of the recording engineer

As with any other art or craft, it takes a long time to learn to be a good recording engineer. But unlike a painter or a musician, the recording engineer has to be content with his or her work going largely unappreciated by the general public. Most people, when they listen to a record, compact disc or tape, hear only the music. The techniques that were employed to record that music at best raise only the merest flicker of interest.

But when you start making recordings yourself, if you have what it takes to be a recording engineer, you begin to hear all sorts of things that at first inspection seem to have nothing to do with the music itself. You hear the ambience of the recording studio, the low 50Hz buzz of a guitar amplifier, snare wires rattling in sympathy with one of the tom toms in the kit. All of these things are actually part of the music too, to the recording engineer. It is not merely the notes played and sung by the musicians that are important, everything that can be heard on the recording is an integral part of the listening experience.

It is in the nature of things that in any field of endeavour some will achieve greatness, some will fail miserably, and the great majority will be average. Take a look at your record or CD collection and you will find that this is true for recording engineers. Chances are that you will be able to pick a couple of discs that, disregarding their musical content, sound really excellent. There are almost certainly a couple that, although you like the music, you just wish they could have been better recorded. But the majority of the records in your collection are almost bound to be in the 'average' category.

What does this mean? One factor of which I am certain is that a few recording engineers are much better at their craft than the rest. Another factor is that on certain album recordings, the interaction between the people involved – musicians, producer, engineer and studio staff – results in them all raising their game beyond their normal abilities on that one project. My theory also implies that there are a lot of people doing an everyday job turning out workmanlike but unexceptional recordings. Let's try and improve a little on that.

Now it is time to listen to some music. Take out a really good sounding album, and one that is average. Have a good listen and compare. Try and pick out all the factors which, to your mind, distinguish the excellent from the run of the mill. Listen really hard to the individual instruments and form an opinion about what they sound like – bright, bassy, fat, thin… there is an almost infinite number of adjectives that can be used to describe sounds. But if you make an effort to put the characteristics of a sound into words, you really have to listen precisely to that sound. Now you are training your engineer's ear.

What is a good recording?

This is not exactly the easiest question in the world to answer. Everyone is entitled to their own opinion, just as everyone is entitled to their own taste in music. But if you are in the business of making and selling recordings, you have to attempt to make some sort of objective judgment – or else how can you assess whether you are coming up with sounds that people will want to buy. The cop-out answer to 'What is a good recording?' is a recording which complements and enhances the music. A sound that suits the Amadeus String Quartet is not necessarily a sound that would suit Guns N'Roses. Another easy answer to the question would be to say that a good frequency response is required, together with low noise and low distortion. But that is a technical answer which is in no way relevant to the art of recording. Great recordings have been made on equipment which is markedly inferior to that which we have available today.

So if we consider, as just one characteristic, the clarity of a recording, then the recording needs to be as clear as the music warrants. If the music is complex, then an open acoustic will probably be beneficial, so that the strands of the musical argument are fully audible. If the music is atmospheric, then a reverberant sound may be more suitable to help the musical lines blend together. But neither of these suggestions are rules. A judgment needs to be made in each individual case. Bearing this in mind, listen to some music carefully and decide whether the recording is not clear enough, just right, or too clear. Try to imagine how it would be if you could reach into the recording studio and turn down the level of the reverberation, or turn it up.

Another recording characteristic is the balance of the instruments. There is no one right way to balance instruments. But the sounds of the particular instruments that are recorded will dictate how the balancing should be done to benefit the music. Listen, on your chosen record, to the balance between the bass guitar or synth and bass drum. How would it sound if one or the other were louder? Being

Get the best result

My idea of a good recording is one which exploits the song fully. Gets the best out of the music, if you like. Any recording technique that helps the music should be used. Conversely, any technique that acts to the detriment of the music should be abandoned. Further than this, I would also say that any recording tricks used purely as 'fixits' – to cover faults – do not help to make a great record. They just bring a below average sound up to par.

able to imagine how things will sound before you alter the settings on the equipment is an important recording engineering skill. The imagination can take a whole series of twists and turns in the time it would take to try out just one adjustment.

Ultimately, a truly objective assessment of the quality of a recording is impossible. But if you listen critically to a large number of recordings, good, average and bad, and decide what particular features of the recording sound good to you, then you will have as objective a reference as it is possible to get when it comes to deciding whether your recordings are up to standard.

What does a recording engineer do?

There are many different types of recording engineer, but here I am going to consider the situation where the engineer works directly with the musicians, without the assistance of a producer. Taking the whole spectrum of recording studios into account, from garage level up, this probably applies to the majority. Also, in situations where one of the musicians considers himself to be the producer of the recording, the fact is that the engineer is probably doing most of the real production work, even if he or she doesn't claim a full share of the credit.

The most basic function of the recording engineer is to make decisions. Decisions about how to go about the next task in the recording, decisions on whether the sounds he is getting are good or bad, and decisions on whether the last take was good enough or needs to be retaken. Sometimes these decisions are straightforward, sometimes not. Often, it doesn't matter what the engineer decides, as long as he plumps firmly for one of the available options – any decision is better than no decision. Of course, the engineer has a series of jobs to do as well, but he is probably the only person present who can tell whether these jobs are being done to the correct standard. Being a recording engineer demands a high level of self motivation.

As well as making decisions and being self motivated, the engineer also has to know how to bring the best out the musicians – especially vocalists. The good engineer has an infinite amount of patience, encouragement, persuasion and tact to offer. It is quite possible that an engineer may be brilliant with sounds, yet lack these personal qualities that are essential to the production of a good recording.

So far, the recording engineer is a decision maker, and a man manager. He is also largely responsible for planning the session and making the best use of the resources of the studio. In fact, planning the session is first thing that should take place before a microphone is plugged in or a fader raised. The engineer needs to know what instruments are to be used, how many tracks will be recorded – the overall shape that the session will take. Even if plans are rather vague at first, or even if the music is to be entirely improvised with no plan at all, the engineer needs to know as much as anyone else does, more in fact, about what is expected to happen.

Of course, the engineer needs to be able to operate the equipment too. But in some ways, technical knowledge is secondary to the factors mentioned above which have a direct bearing on the quality of musical performance. Good engineering can enhance good music, it can't transmute base metal into a potential gold disc. I comment on these non-technical aspects a) because they are extremely important and b) because the following chapters will concentrate on recording studio procedures and operating the equipment. If I could include a chapter on how to develop tact, patience and the other qualities I have mentioned I would, but I am afraid you will have to look to your own resources for these.

Starting at the front end of the recording, the engineer is responsible for the selection of the correct microphone for each instrument, and for its positioning. Of course, many recordings are now made by plugging a synth or sampler straight into the mixing console. But the option of going through a microphone is still available, simply by plugging the synth into an amp and speaker, and it has a definite value. The range of sound qualities offered by microphone selection and placement is infinitely wide. Each engineer learns by experience which mic suits which instrument. There are no rules, and opinions differ. As far as mic placement goes, there are a few simple guidelines, which I shall be looking into, but the right position is always the position where the mic sounds good, regardless of theory.

If a group of instruments are being recorded simultaneously, then the engineer tells the players where to sit, and may position acoustic screens where necessary. A symphony orchestra will have some pretty definite ideas on how it likes to be arranged, but nevertheless the engineer is responsible for getting a good recording and must have his say so that a good compromise can be reached.

When recording an instrument to multitrack tape, there are a number of options. The engineer may decide to add equalisation and effects as part of the track or simply record the instrument 'dry' for later treatment. Each procedure has its merits and demerits. The recording level on tape is vitally important to getting a clean noise-free recording. Perhaps the most mundane task an engineer has is 'nursing' a fader during a lengthy overdub session, but that is his job and he must get it right.

If the studio is making enough profit to employ an assistant engineer, then the control of the multitrack tape machine may be out of the engineer's domain. But he will still be in charge of which instrument goes on which track, and make sure that a record – a 'track sheet' – is kept for reference throughout the recording. The engineer, whether or not he operates the multitrack, will also find himself responsible if a track is inadvertently over-recorded, erasing something that might have taken hours to create. Needless to say, this is a great responsibility, and generally speaking accidental erasure only happens once in an engineer's career (the session on which it happens may mark his retirement!).

As recording and overdubbing proceeds, the engineer is watching out for anything that might be detrimental to the quality of the end product. It could be a combination of sounds that will not mix well later, or a slightly fluffed note, perhaps acceptable to a musician who is more used to live work, but the engineer is attuned to faults that will become annoying on repeated listening. The engineer, whether or not he is a musician himself, will also be continually assessing the state of tune of the instruments. Although tuning should be the musicians' job, the engineer will be listening very closely to the sound and may pick up a slight tuning problem before anyone else. And since poor tuning can ruin a recording, the engineer must speak up.

For monitoring during overdubs, the engineer must provide a monitor mix, so he and the musicians can judge what is being, and has already been, recorded. The monitor mix may be very close to the eventual final mix, or it may be purely a working arrangement, with very approximate levels. A foldback mix is used for musicians listening on headphones while they overdub a new track. Sometimes two or more different foldback mixes are required. Foldback mixes can often be a bad pain in the engineer's neck.

When the multitrack recording is complete, the engineer will construct a rough mix, probably unassisted. Then the various parties who have an interest in the recording will want to have their say. If the members of a five piece band all want to make an input, finding the right mix may be difficult. The important thing is to consider the requirements of the music, not the requirements of the bass player who wants to be louder than everyone else to satisfy his own vanity. For the final mix onto stereo tape or DAT, the engineer will attend to changes in balance as the mix progresses, and also make sure the level on the tape is correct. When complete, he will leader up the tape and, most importantly, label the box, or the DAT cassette and inlay card. Even if an assistant completes these tasks, it will be the engineer's fault if there is a problem later on – through incorrect labelling for example.

When the session is finished, the engineer or his assistant can tidy up the studio, reset all the controls on the mixing console to zero, and count the microphones to make sure none has gone astray. Since it is by now about 3 o'clock in the morning, it is time to get some rest ready for an 11 a.m. start next day.

This is just an outline of the recording engineer's role, which I shall expand upon in the following chapters as I describe many of the range of recording studio operations.

Microphone techniques

2

However convenient it may be to direct-inject an electric guitar or bass, or plug a synthesiser straight to one of the console's line inputs, there is a certain something about a sound produced by the natural vibration of timber or metal that travels through the air and finds its way to the tape via a microphone. One of the negative aspects of today's synth and sampler based techniques is that recordings tend to have a 'samey' quality about them. After all, one man's 'M1 Piano' cannot be very far removed from another's. In an ideal world – i.e. a world constructed for the benefit of creating quality music – there would be no presets and synths would be supplied like blank sheets of paper for their owners to write upon in their particular sonic handwriting. In the real world, manufacturers have to create presets to show off what their gear can do, and it is only human nature that most of us end up using them.

Recording real sounds with a microphone is another matter entirely. There are so many variables it is almost impossible for two recordings to sound exactly alike. Of course, an acoustic guitar will always tend to sound like an acoustic guitar, but not nearly to the same extent that Factory Preset 56 in Tartan Studio, John O'Groats, will sound like Factory Preset 56 in Laidback Studio, Los Angeles. Let's look at just what these variables may be when you record with a microphone:

First, the instrument. If you play any acoustic instrument, you will know that no two models are the same. Even if they came off the same production line on the same day, after a few month's wear and tear they will perform and sound differently. This is the same as saying that every instrument has its own character. Assuming that we are talking about an acoustic guitar for the moment, another variable is the brand of strings used, and their age. As a new set of strings settles in the tone changes from twangy to bright to mellow to dull to time to get a new set! The type of plectrum used affects the sound too, whether it is thick or thin, stiff or flexible.

As well as the guitar, another important factor is the guitarist. There is a world of difference between the sound of Mr. Average

Guitarist playing a simple E chord, and a master virtuoso. Compare that to the case of an electronic keyboard where a note played by a master would not sound any different to a note played by a monkey.

Still on the subject of variables, but looking from the engineer's angle, just as all instruments are different, all microphones are different. Two mics may be very very similar when new, but like instruments they will age differently. Microphone diaphragms get dirty and different types of studios produce different types of dirt.

The most important variable factors in acoustic recording are the studio and the engineer. All studios and rooms sound different, and different parts of the same room will have a different acoustic. It is one of the engineer's jobs to position the instrument and microphone appropriately, not just in relation to each other, but in relation to the room. Imagine the simple situation of one instrument, one mic and one room. Now imagine how many different ways they could be physically arranged to make a recording. When a synthesiser manufacturer says that his instrument has 'an infinite range of sounds', he is obviously seriously underestimating the concept of infinity.

So far, I have been talking about purely acoustic instruments. But the electric guitar can be an acoustic instrument too – if it is plugged into an amp and speaker so it can be recorded via a microphone. Once again, there is a tremendous increase in the range of sounds that can be obtained over simple direct inject techniques. Even with synths and samplers, there is no reason why they should not be amplified and miked up. It all makes for greater diversity.

Microphone types

Not all microphones are suitable for making recordings. But the good news is that most modern types are! As microphone technology improves, quality mics are to be found at lower and lower prices – but obviously there is a limit beyond which you are not going to get much satisfaction, unless you are aiming for a special effect. The choice of microphone that will be used for a recording is very much an artistic choice. In other fields of sound engineering there may be other important factors such as size, appearance, robustness. But as a recording engineer, you have a free choice among all the different types of mic you can lay your hands on.

There are several different basic microphone designs that need explanation, they all have different sound characters and will find different uses. The main categories are capacitor and dynamic. There is also a type of capacitor mic called an 'electret' and a type of dynamic mic known as a 'ribbon'. The capacitor microphone is blessed with a very clear sound, rich in high frequencies. The dynamic mic is usually

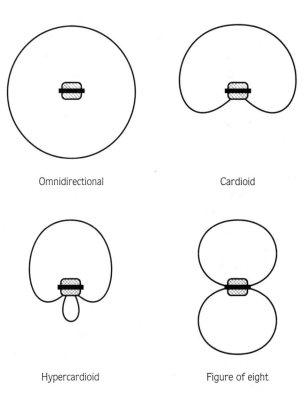

Fig 2.1 Microphone polar patterns

Omnidirectional   Cardioid

Hypercardioid   Figure of eight

less clear, but can give 'body' to the sound when used appropriately.

Both capacitor and dynamic mics are available with different 'polar patterns'. The polar pattern of a mic describes its sensitivity in different directions, the four main types being Omnidirectional, Cardioid, Hypercardioid and Figure of Eight. Figure 2.1 shows the possibilities, bearing in mind that these are two-dimensional sketches of patterns that exist in the three-dimensional real world.

The major factor accounting for the sound quality of any microphone is frequency response. A good quality microphone pointing directly at a sound source will have a frequency response similar to that shown in Figure 2.2. As you can see, the frequency response is very nearly flat. The slight rise in the high frequency range is due to reflections from the diaphragm interacting with the incoming sound. In good quality mics, this tendency is well under control. But the 'on-axis' frequency response, as it is called, is one thing. The 'off-axis' response is entirely another. The top manufacturers can make mics with ruler flat on-axis responses that will capture the particular balance of frequencies produced by any instrument perfectly. But the frequency response to sound sources which are not precisely in the mic's 'line of fire' is, for all manufacturers, a tougher problem.

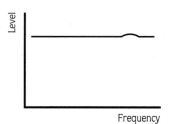

Fig 2.2 Typical on-axis frequency response

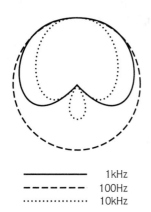

————————	1kHz
– – – – – – –	100Hz
·················	10kHz

Fig 2.3 The polar patterns at different frequencies of a nominally cardioid mic

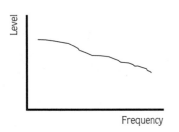

Fig 2.4 Typical off-axis frequency response

Figure 2.3 shows the polar pattern of a typical microphone at three different frequencies. At 1kHz, you will see that it corresponds to the cardioid pattern shown in Figure 2.1. But at high frequency, the response tends towards the hypercardioid – it becomes more directional – and at low frequencies it tends towards omni. Shown as an off-axis frequency response plot, the result is Figure 2.4. This is not a flat frequency response by any standards, and even very high quality mics have this problem. But you may say that if you are pointing the mic directly at the sound source, then the off-axis response doesn't matter. Well, this is true if you are recording at a distance from the source in the open air, or in an anechoic chamber. But in a real room or studio, the reflections from walls, floor and ceiling make a significant contribution to the quality of the sound. If this quality is affected by the microphone, then the recording will have less than perfect fidelity to the original. You could say that the recording will have 'character' if you wanted to put a more positive emphasis on the situation.

If I were to define what makes a 'good' mic, then I would say that a flat on-axis frequency response coupled with a good off-axis response is the thing to have. Alternatively, a good mic could also be defined as one that has the right sort of character, rather than a perfect response. By 'character' I mean an interesting combination of defects! Some mics I could name have defects in abundance but sound great. They don't capture a sound with perfect fidelity, but the way in which they change the sound is musically useful. One story I was told by a BBC engineer a few years ago is that they like to use old-fashioned ribbon mics for their World Service broadcasts because they can cover more square miles on the other side of the world with good intelligibility than they can using more modern, more 'accurate', types.

One particular 'defect' which is worthy of mention is present in microphones which have a large diaphragm (the diaphragm is the mic's 'ear drum'). All diaphragms will tend to have a resonant frequency – a frequency at which they will naturally vibrate – which colours the sound. In small diaphragm mics, this resonant frequency will be above the audio band and thus will be to all intents and purposes inaudible. There are many mics in popular use that have a diaphragm an inch or more across and have their resonance in the audio band. The effect on frequency response this may have is controllable, but the colouration isn't – at least not totally. But very often this is exactly what engineers are looking for – something that makes the sound more interesting and alive. Many antique microphones that, in theory, should have been superseded eons ago are still in common day-to-day use while super accurate high-tech models are lounging in their foam nests in the mic cupboard.

Technique

'Microphone technique' is a phrase that conjures up an image of a veteran recording engineer lecturing his young trainee about exactly where to point the microphone for every instrument ever invented, as if there are laws laid down by Act of Parliament. From my own experience as a sound engineer, and from my involvement with other engineers, I know that mics that work for one person, and methods that work for one person, don't necessarily work for another. I have my favourite microphones and I like to think that I can get a good sound from them in a variety of circumstances. There are other mics that I just don't seem to be able to get a usable sound out of, but I have heard recordings made by other engineers, using those same mics, which are brilliant.

Although there are no rules on microphone technique, I can give some hints on how to go about miking up instruments in general. The first thing to do, when approached with an acoustic instrument to record is to engage the brain in first gear and gently release the clutch! A little thought can go a long way towards getting the sound you want to hear.

Instruments, as you know, come in a variety of shapes and sizes, from the tiny piccolo to the six feet tall double bass. Each instrument radiates a sound field in its own particular way. An acoustic guitar, for example radiates a thin metallic sound from the strings, a middle frequency sound from the body, and a mellow tone from the sound hole. So, point-to-remember No. 1 is that all instruments emit different types of sound from different parts of their bodies. Another example is the flute which has a breathy sound when miked close to the player's lips and a more mellow sound from other parts of the instrument. Any mic position may be suitable for the music you are recording, it is up to you to experiment.

All instruments sound different according to the distance between mic and instrument. There are two reasons for this. The first is that the further away the mic is from the instrument, the more reverberation or ambience will be picked up from the room. That is fairly obvious. The less obvious point is that since all parts of the instrument radiate with a different sound quality, the further away you get from the instrument, the more you pick up the sound from its entire body, and integrate these different sounds.

To put this in is as neat a nutshell as I can manage, if you want a natural sound, use the mic at a distance of at least 1.5 times the maximum dimension of the instrument. This will pick up the instrument as the ear normally would. But for a sound with 'character', place the microphone close to the instrument. Different parts of the instrument will have a different sound quality.

There is one more aspect to the distance between instrument and microphone that deserves consideration. The amount of room ambience that will be picked up at any given distance depends on the polar pattern of the mic. An omnidirectional microphone will pick up much more room sound than a hypercardioid at the same distance. This is a simple point, and is explained very quickly, but it is very important to be aware of this when positioning the mic.

Microphone technique, to summarise, is not a set of hard and fast rules to be followed. It is something that you learn as you progress as an engineer, and will probably develop differently to other engineers. The only rule is to experiment. That way you will find the techniques that suit you. Eventually you will develop a mental database of techniques and will be able very quickly to get the precise sound you want from any instrument.

Multiple microphones

Put two people together in the same room for any length of time and an argument will develop, sooner or later. Like people, microphones argue too. Two identical microphones picking up one sound source will hear the sound differently simply because they are at different points in space. Often, mixing the sounds from the mics produces a worse sound than using just one mic. But sometimes multiple mics can be beneficial, and sometimes essential. A favourite technique of many engineers is to use a close mic and a distant mic at the same time to combine the clarity of the former with the warmth of the latter. This doesn't cause too many problems because the two mics are picking up sounds which are very different. Just experiment with the mic positions and mix to taste.

The classic source of multi-mic problems is recording a drum kit. Recording drums is probably the most difficult situation an engineer ever has to face simply because of the number of mics active at the same time. But why use a lot of mics on a drum kit? In the early days of recording, one microphone might have been considered adequate for recording the kit. In those days it was adequate, because that particular technique suited the sounds and styles of the period. One mic, or a pair for stereo, on a drum kit can produce a very good representation of what the kit sounds like in real life.

Today's recordings demand extreme clarity from each drum and cymbal. To get this clarity we need to use a mic on each drum, a mic on the hihat and two overhead mics to pick up the cymbals. Even in a small kit that amounts to eight or so mics. Unfortunately, clarity is reduced by the fact that every mic picks up every drum and cymbal to some extent. When all the mics are mixed together this can result in a horrible mush that sounds less clear and distinct than using just one mic.

The solution is to use directional mics and place them close to the drums. There is a simple rule that there must be a ten-to-one ratio between the distance of the mic that is intended to pick up a particular drum and the distance of the next closest mic. Some negotiation with the drummer may make this possible. If the mixing console has a phase reverse button on each channel, it is often worthwhile playing about with the phase of the various mics. Sometimes the complex interaction between the distances of the mics and the frequencies produced by the drums may cause phase cancellations that may be at least partially curable by a bit of button pushing. Of course, there is a lot more to recording drums than this, but these are the basics and everything else builds on top. For the moment, I shall ignore problems that might occur with the kit itself, and leave them, along with some more sophisticated drum recording techniques, until Chapter 7.

There is a whole world of experience waiting for the engineer who wishes to get his hands dirty and abandon the nice clean world of direct inject synths and samplers. So far, I have covered the fundamentals of the subject, but there is much more to know. Later I shall be passing on more microphone related hints. But the best thing to do is to experiment and find out how many creative possibilities there are in the acoustic world.

Stereo recording

There are some classical techniques for simple stereo recording, all of which have been well tried and tested. Figure 2.5 shows the 'Crossed Pair' which can be used with all types of mic except omnidirectional. Since both mics are in the same place, the stereo effect depends on the mic pointing to the left picking up more level on sounds coming from the left hand side of the sound stage than the mic on the right. This configuration produces a clear stereo image which is mono compatible, although it doesn't give the feeling of 'spaciousness' that other techniques offer.

Figure 2.6 shows the 'Spaced Omni' technique which is sometimes supplemented with a centre mic. Despite having omni in the name, it can be used with all types of mic. This technique does not give precisely localised images, but does give a full 'spacious' sound. Usually, it doesn't combine as well into mono as the Crossed Pair.

Figure 2.7 shows a combination of the two – the 'Spaced Crossed Pair' to give it an unofficial title. With a separation between the mics

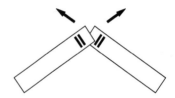

Fig 2.5 Crossed pair of directional microphones. Figure of eight mics should cross at 90 degrees, cardioids theoretically at 120 degrees

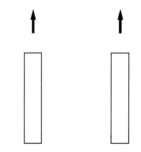

Fig 2.6 Spaced omni arrangement. Separation is from about 1 metre up to about half of the 'sound stage'

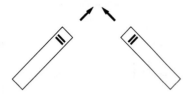

Fig 2.7 Spaced crossed pair of microphones

of a few centimetres it gives all the advantages of the Crossed Pair with added spaciousness. It can be used successfully with a spacing of up to around a foot. Any more than that and it approximates to the Spaced Omni technique but risks losing instruments placed centre stage. In Figure 2.7 you may notice that the mic on the left is actually pointing right and the mic on the right is pointing left. Some engineers would say that this is incorrect and it ought to be arranged so that the left hand mic points left and right points right. Well practice is very often at odds with theory and the sound of this arrangement can indeed be good.

Bass 'Tip Up'

Any microphone, other than an omnidirectional type, will exhibit the phenomenon sometimes called bass tip-up when placed close to the sound source. This is due to the curvature of the sound wavefront, which is more marked at a close distance from the source, and the way in which it interacts with the diaphragm. Often, the more bassy sound offered by a close non-omni mic (i.e. cardioid, hypercardioid or figure of eight) is 'warmer' and preferable to a strictly flat response. The engineer will take this into account when choosing a mic.

Musical arrange-
ment for recording

M usic is the recording engineer's raw material. Even the best engineer can't make a good recording unless the music is up to scratch. Music, one might say, is made up of three components: the notes, the arrangement and the performance. In this chapter I am going to concentrate on the very relevant topic of musical arrangement. The arrangement of any piece of music is as important as are the musical ideas themselves. Think of it as a language that helps those ideas get clearly across to the listener.

Let's look at exactly what an arrangement is, and then examine how arranging techniques are of interest both in the performance of music and to the recording engineer. Imagine a songwriter or composer sitting at a piano, thrashing out notes, probably humming a tune at the same time, and scribbling away on a sheet of music manuscript paper. What he or she writes is probably as close as you can get to the notion of a musical idea in its pure form. Strictly speaking, what is written down is a piano arrangement, but it bears the same relationship to a fully developed arrangement as a storyboard sequence of sketches bears to a motion picture in full Technicolor.

From a sketched piano arrangement, an arranger or orchestrator could build up a full score for a whole orchestra. The notes in the piano arrangement would all appear in the score, distributed among the various instruments, but the arranger would flesh out these few notes with ideas of his own, thus developing the composer's rough idea into into a fully worked out composition. The old-time great composers were, on the whole, their own arrangers. But it is now very common for composing and arranging to be individualised tasks.

Sometimes, arranging isn't a process that is thought about consciously. The arrangement may be, more or less, dictated by the combination of instruments used. For example, the archetypal pop group line up, dating back to the fifties and sixties is two guitars, bass guitar and drums. In a group like this, the roles of the instruments are pretty well fixed. Each musician plays what seems appropriate for the song, and the arrangement develops without anyone having to take it upon himself to organise.

Arrangement essentials

Any musical arrangement will have six basic features, all present to a greater or lesser extent. These are: Melody, Harmony, Bass, Motion, Rhythm and Decoration. These are not standard textbook headings, but they will help me to explain how arrangements are built up.

Melody

A tune is – obviously – a sequence of single notes. But think about what those notes are doing. They are telling a story, leading from one note to another, forming a pattern which lingers for a short time in the memory, until a new pattern begins. A good tune - even a mediocre tune - has a quality which makes you want to continue listening until the next note, and the next, and so on. The melody may be the raison d'etre of a piece of music, or may be used as a constructional device to assist another more important feature.

Harmony

Back in the mists of musical history, there was a time when harmony hadn't been invented. The best they could do was for everyone to sing the tune in unison or in octaves. Harmony is like a room in which the melody lives. It may be a comfortably furnished room, or it may be austere. Sometimes it is a vacant room – there is no melody within.

Bass

The bass is the foundation on which the rest of the arrangement stands. But it may take on aspects of melody and harmony. It will probably also contribute to...

Motion

Motion is my term for the elements of an arrangement which, apart from the melody, drive the music forward. This may be done by skillful use of the harmony and bass, or motion may be achieved with a specially dedicated musical line.

Rhythm

Rhythm is not the same as motion, but is one of the elements that might create it. Rhythm means repetition – of drum or percussion patterns perhaps, or maybe just a sequence of accented notes.

Decoration

When the arrangement is built up and is functioning properly, additional layers of decoration may be applied. They are not structurally vital, but they add surface glitter and ear-appeal.

Let's apply these six features to the simple two guitars, bass and drums line up and see how they work:

In the case of a song, the melody will simply be the vocal line, so that's soon dealt with. The main harmony of the arrangement is provided by one of the guitars, traditionally called the rhythm guitar, playing chords to suit the melody. The bass is – of course – provided by the bass guitar and rhythm by the drums. Apart from the drums, where does the motion in the arrangement come from? If the rhythm and bass guitars play just one chord plus bass note per bar, then there won't be much motion. Motion is created by the rhythm guitar strumming, and the bass guitar playing extra notes which are not strictly essential to the support of the harmony.

Decoration is the responsibility of the lead guitarist, who plays 'licks' and counter melodies, and the drummer who plays a 'fill' every so often, probably at the ends of the musical phrases. The guitars/bass/drums line up didn't develop by accident, as you can see. It can provide all the features that a musical arrangement must have, albeit at a fairly simple level with a minimum of instrumentation. Providing one or more members of the band can sing, this combination can produce a full, satisfying sound.

Another combination of instruments that didn't just come about by chance is the symphony orchestra. Orchestral music may not be to everyone's taste, but arrangement-wise it has much in common with modern styles. The standard symphony orchestra has four instrumental sections: strings, woodwind, brass and percussion. Of these four sections, the busiest is usually the strings. (One reason for this is that it takes a lot more energy to play a wind instrument and the players need to rest during the performance). The strings of the orchestra – violin, viola, cello and double bass – cover the full range of the spectrum of useful musical notes, they are capable of a wide range of dynamics and can play in a variety of styles. Because of this versatility, many orchestral arrangements use the strings as the basis of the music, and the other instruments as a contrast or as reinforcement.

Some particular instruments of the orchestra have particular roles and do not depart much from them: The French horn, in its earlier days before it had valves, was often used to 'hold' the music together. While the strings and other wind instruments were playing the musically interesting parts. The horns played long sustained notes which had the effect of binding the string and wind sounds together. The piccolo, a half size flute, is rarely used on its own. It has a very bright, piercing timbre, and when the full orchestra is belting out a fortissimo passage, the piccolo is still clearly heard, and gives the sound a cutting edge. The timpani are tuned kettle drums nestling among the other instruments of the percussion section. They have two functions – to provide accents in loud exciting passages, and played softly to add atmosphere and mystery when the music is quiet.

Even if you don't have access to a symphony orchestra to perform your music, modern instruments such as guitars, synths and samplers fulfil many of the same functions as orchestral instruments. The basic way in which music works is still the same.

Recording arrangements

Once upon a time, recording - even multitrack recording – meant capturing an existing performing arrangement on tape where the musicians had worked out what they were going to play. They were probably capable of performing the piece perfectly well live on stage and simply recreated their live performance in the studio, with extra precision and perhaps with a little extra decoration. Recording, as it is practised today, is much more involved with building up the arrangement as the recording progresses. That's why a knowledge of arranging techniques is important to the engineer. When finished, the recording will have to fulfil a number of criteria. Whether it succeeds will depend on the arrangement at least as much as the engineering skill and the recording techniques employed.

Apart from matching the mood of the song or piece of music, the arrangement should provide a sound which is adequately full - not a sparse sound, lacking in substance. Fullness can, to a certain extent, be enhanced by appropriate recording techniques, but it is mainly down to the arrangement to achieve this. The arrangement should also be interesting, with the appropriate amount of decoration but not so much as to clutter the music. The sounds of the individual instruments should integrate so that they blend together well, and they should provide a good balance between the high and low end of the frequency spectrum. One further point is that the listener's interest in the music should not diminish during the course of the piece. It may, and it is a function of the arrangement to make sure that it doesn't.

Although I have so far been commenting on the instrumentation of an arrangement, another important factor in arranging something like a song is to get the musical structure correct even before thinking about instruments. Sometimes, this doesn't apply because the structure cannot be changed. It is not customary, for instance, to alter the structure of a classical piece in a simple arrangement. But when the options are open it really pays to think about which bit of music goes where, whether the song should start with a verse or chorus, would a different introduction be better, how should it end?. There are lots of things to think about.

Going back to the instrumental content of the music, let's imagine that a song is being recorded on multitrack from scratch, adding musical lines instrument by instrument as seems appropriate. I'll start with some basic building blocks:

Since it's a song, then the instrument responsible for the melody line is already fixed – the voice. To support the melody there must be a bass, for now just the minimum amount of notes to tie in with the vocal line. A simple way of adding motion and rhythm would be drums. Notice how I am setting out what I want to achieve, and then how I intend to achieve it. It's obvious in the case of drums, but later on there may be options.

Drummers, or drum machine programmers, use two very powerful methods for propelling the rhythm forwards: the off-beat snare and the hihat pulse. Almost any pop, rock or jazz piece of music uses these two techniques because they are so straightforward and so powerful. To emphasise the off-beat snare, a bass drum beat is added at the beginning of each bar. This is really getting down to the nitty gritty of musical arrangement to think about the function of each beat in a drum pattern, but it's much better to know why something is done than just to do it because that's the way everyone else does.

Two other drum tricks: Instead of having bass drum on beat 1 and snare on beat 3 of a four beat bar, put a bass drum pulse on each beat. And/or, make a hihat pattern of 16th notes, with an accent on the third pulse of each group of four. Trevor Horn, producer of Frankie Goes to Hollywood and many others, made a mint out of this one back in the 1980s, and it has come back many times since.

Now we are getting somewhere with melody, bass and rhythm, the rhythm supplying some of the necessary motion. Next on the list is harmony. The standard arrangement trick for filling out the harmony of a track is to use a pad. Once again, the pad is a simple idea, but it works. There are other ways to achieve the same, but the pad is definitely the most used.

So what is a pad? Just a straight series of chords played on a sustaining instrument to the harmony required by the tune. No movement, no interesting features, just bland straight chords. Commonly requested types of pad are the 'string pad' which could be real strings, but is more often a synth playing a string patch. It doesn't usually sound much like real strings, but it has a similar texture and

Tricky business

Here's a little trick that's useful when the rhythm of a song seems to sag halfway though, perhaps because the phrase lengths are too regular and the ear has become just a little jaded. The trick is to miss something out, a beat or a bar. If a song consists of regular eight bar phrases, cut one phrase to seven bars towards the end of the song. Or cut the last eighth note (quaver) from the last bar of the phrase. Both, if applied suitably, will have the effect of throwing the song forward, increasing its momentum and making the ear prick up.
An analogous technique, which has perhaps been a little over used, is to change key either a tone or a semitone upwards towards the end to give the song a lift. It's a cliche, but it works.

harmonises and fills out the song at the same time. The 'Rhodes pad' is similar but done on a Fender Rhodes piano, preferably with a chorus effect, or nowadays its synthesised or sampled alternative. Since a piano sound doesn't sustain like strings, the notes are unobtrusively repeated.

There are other alternatives to the string or Rhodes pad, in fact any bland sustaining sound will do. Sometimes a pad with more character is used, so much that it becomes interesting in its own right. The Pet Shop Boys' 'West End Girls' is a fine example of this, where the pad sounds like – but probably isn't – a rusty old Mellotron with a severe case of moth infestation. It wouldn't suit every track, but it suits that one.

The beauty of the pad is that it provides a base for subsequent musical parts to work on. It's like an artist applying a basic wash of colour to his canvas before adding in the detail with a fine brush. Sometimes, as recording progresses, you find that the pad has served its purpose. You have built up enough extra layers, each having different musical details, to give a full sound without a pad.

Our track now has a full sound, but it has only rhythmic motion. It needs musical motion too to give it direction. With the existing instrumentation, this can be done by making the bass more mobile with extra harmony and passing notes. Another simple way is to add some more chords, but now with some rhythmic interest. A neat trick to add motion is to have a 16th note pulse, either chords or single notes, running through the song. This always works, but you can't do it in every song or it becomes an easy way out, a substitute for creative thought.

On top of this basic structure goes the decoration to provide the necessary interest. The decoration can be pretty well anything: extra instruments, contrasting combinations of instruments, changes of instrumental timbre, syncopated rhythms etc etc. A good decorative device, which also helps pull the song along, is the counter melody. This is a melody, probably instrumental rather than vocal, which runs together with the main tune but where the main tune 'ebbs and flows', the counter melody should 'flow and ebb', maintaining the overall level of activity.

One last technique I can mention is employed in just about every track recorded – the 'build up', or simply 'build'. With an unchanging combination of instruments, even a very well arranged combination, repetition will gradually produce boredom. One way to get around this is to use different combinations of instruments over the duration of the piece. This is good for lengthy classical pieces, but not for a modern song recording. One of the typical aims of a song recording is to create a single atmosphere or mood that lasts for three minutes without really changing at all. There are tracks that are more complex, Phil Collins' 'In the Air Tonight' being a good example of a song with two distinctly different sections. But if, as usual, the song has to retain the same feel throughout, then you can't chop and change instruments or sounds.

The answer is to start the track fairly simply, and add more and more interest as the song progresses, as the ear gets bored with what it has already heard. By the end of the song, the arrangement can often be quite complex with much decoration – with decoration in the vocal line too. It builds up, in other words.

I can't list every arranging trick and technique, because there are probably millions of them. That's why there are specialist arrangers who can command their pay through a good knowledge of how to get the best out of a piece of music. But the main trick is to know what you want to achieve, and to acquire, through experiment and practice, a range of techniques to allow you to do that. Listening to the arrangement of a track that you think is musically successful is bound to help. But don't forget that sometimes what works for one person may not necessarily work for another. Develop your own arranging skills and techniques and perhaps you will come up with a completely new and original sound.

4 Four-track recording

There are three ways to learn about multitrack recording techniques. The first is to be lucky enough to land a job as a trainee - they used to call them tape ops – in a recording studio. With a desire to learn, contact with helpful knowledgeable engineers and an ability to work all hours for minimal pay, there is a direct road to potential success for the fortunate few. The recommended starting point is to make contact with as many recording studios as you can (see list in Chapter 18) and hope that your letter falls on the manager's desk at the very moment a vacancy arises, or go to your local Careers Office who, you may be surprised to find, will be very open minded on the subject. Obviously your chances are better if you live in the big city, the bigger the better.

The second way to learn about recording is to find yourself a training course. There are quite a few about these days, look out for their adverts. Be warned that some courses are very expensive. The third way to get into multitrack recording, and perhaps the most accessible, is to buy yourself a cassette based multitrack recorder. If you already have an instrument or two, or your mates have, then you could start producing demo recordings for a not unreasonable sum of money. There are some multitrackers (as I shall refer to cassette-based four track recorders, for want of a better name other than Portastudio, which is Tascam's trade mark) right at the entry level which give excellent sound quality – but you'll have to pick them out from those that are not quite so hot.

In this chapter, I hope to explain exactly what these multitrackers are, what they do, and the basic techniques you need to get a good result. These basic techniques will still be useful as you progress up the scale to eight, sixteen and hopefully eventually twenty-four track recording.

Design

Let's look for a moment at the design of the cassette tape itself. It certainly wasn't designed for multitrack recording, although it has ultimately proved itself in this application. The original idea behind the cassette was to be able to record fairly low quality stereo sound on both sides of the cassette. As you know, after the first side you can turn it over and start recording again. This means that there are four separate tracks of audio on a normal cassette, but the tracks on Side 2 run in the opposite direction to those on Side 1.

The multitracker uses a head with four record/playback elements stacked up so all four tracks can be recorded in the same direction spread across the full width of the tape. Since the full width is used on each multitrack recording you make, it is not possible to turn the cassette over. Well you can, but you will hear all four tracks running backwards.

Although with modern design and noise reduction techniques, normal stereo cassettes can give a fairly good sound, they are working right at the limits of the magnetic tape medium. Any slight wear or misalignment results in that well known muffled and uneven cassette sound. Most multitrackers get round this with a simple dodge – they run the tape at twice the normal speed. This really does give a great improvement in the stability and consistency of the sound. It means that the tape is eaten up twice as quickly though, and what started out as a C90 cassette on a normal stereo machine ends up as a cassette which lasts only twenty-two and a half minutes – enough for about four songs. It's a good job that cassettes are reasonably cheap these days. And while I'm talking about cheap, it is important not to go too cheap but to buy the correct type of cassette for your machine. This means a Type II variety like TDK SA or equivalent. Your machine's manual will tell you what's best. The sort of things that you will be doing with your multitracker will demand a lot of the tape. If you weigh up the amount of time you put into your recording, and the cost of the tape, then it makes sense to buy the best.

Besides running at twice normal speed, the other quality enhancer used on multitrackers is noise reduction. For ordinary stereo cassettes, Dolby B is the de facto standard. It works very well with a properly aligned machine in a good state of repair. With multitrackers, Dolby B doesn't reduce the noise level nearly enough, only by about 10 decibels. Dolby C and dbx are the systems generally in use. Dolby C, found on Fostex multitrackers, gives a very clean sound. dbx, commonly used by Tascam, Yamaha and others, gives less noise during quiet sections, but is not as transparent while the music is playing. As always, the best advice is to listen for yourself and decide what's best for your sort of music.

Two types

The evolution of the multitracker has split into two lines, one of which more or less follows conventional recording studio practice, and the other is dedicated purely to budget 4-track operation. The former is, obviously, a better education into multitrack ways and will provide a springboard of basic knowledge from which to leap to more advanced systems. The other system is less expensive to implement, and hence is found on less expensive machines. It can still produce excellent results.

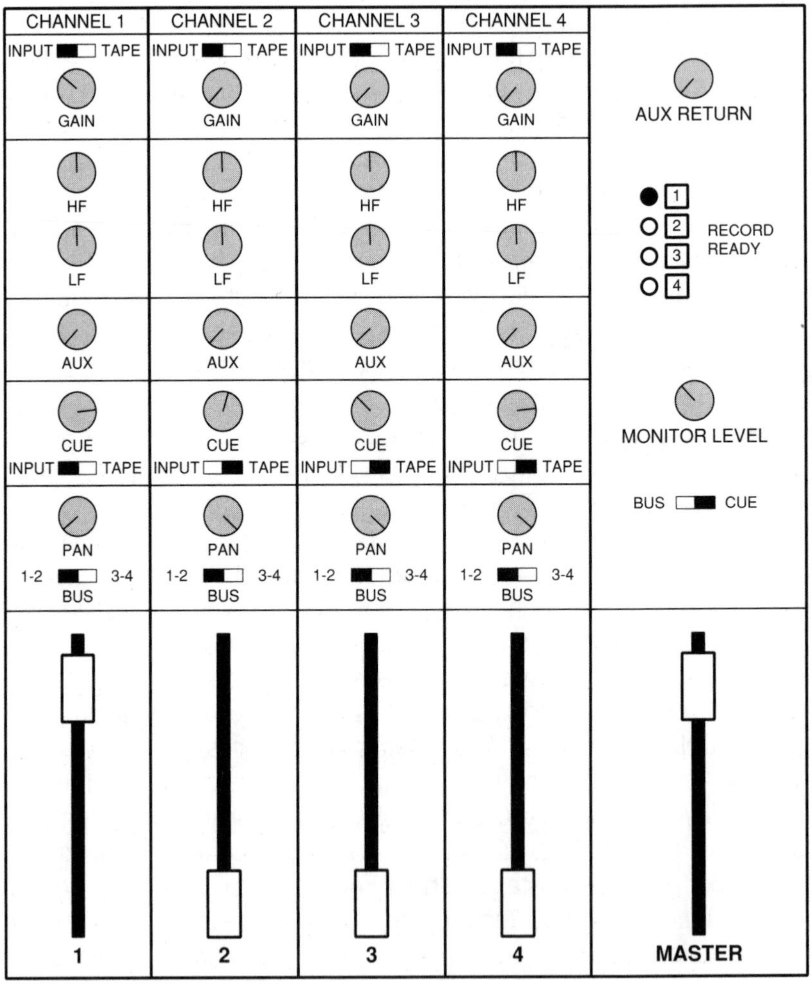

Fig 4.1 A typical 4-track cassette control panel, here set to record on track 1 from channel 1 while monitoring the other three tracks. Transport controls and metering are not shown

Figure 4.1 shows the first type of multitracker (the distinguishing feature being that it has one set of equalisation controls per input channel). It's like a recording studio in miniature with all the features you would expect arranged in a similar way. This isn't a diagram of any particular model, but it has the typical features you would like to find on a high end machine. As you come down the various manufacturers' ranges you will find that some features are dropped, and some are combined with others making the machine less versatile.

Model 1, as I shall call it, combines a four channel mixer with a four track cassette tape recorder, all in one box. Starting with the input channels, at the top of each channel is a gain control. This boosts the signal from whatever level it happens to be, from mic or instrument, up to a level suitable for further processing. Not all multitrackers have gain controls, some have a choice of line input (low gain for a strong signal) or mic input (high gain for a weak signal). Below the gain control is a switch that takes the input to the channel from the input connector or from the output of the cassette. Switch to input when you are recording an instrument on this channel. Switch to tape when you want to monitor the tape track whose number is the same as that of the channel.

The EQ controls tailor the sound that's coming in to your particular requirements. Here I have shown only two fixed frequency controls per channel with variable cut and boost. Sophisticated machines can have variable frequency too. Notice that my Model 1 has four EQ sections, one for each channel. The alternative type of multitracker has just two EQ sections configured in a rather different way.

The aux (auxiliary) send is an extra mixed output from the mixer section. The auxes of all four channels are mixed together and emerge from a connector on the rear panel. The most frequent use for the aux send is to send signal to a reverb unit, as mentioned later.

The cue control is for listening to the signal in the channel, independent of the level going down to tape. You can either monitor the input signal, or whatever is recorded on the corresponding track of the tape.

This unit has four mix buses and a bus select switch. Each mix bus is simply a piece of wire, or copper track on the printed circuit board, that picks up signal from any or all of the channels and takes it along to a single tape track. Four buses obviously correspond to four tracks. Here the switch sets the channel to Buses 1 and 2, or 3 and 4. This means that if you select 1 and 2, the pan control pans the signal between Track 1 and Track 2 of the tape. If the pan is set all the way to the left, the signal goes to Track 1. If the pan is all the way to the right, it goes to Track 2. With the pan control centred, the signal goes equally to both tracks.

Some multitrackers only have two buses. You can still record on all four tracks (it would be pointless if you couldn't!), but you are restricted to recording only two tracks at a time. This is not so good for recording bands playing live, although individual types of two bus multitracker may have ways of getting around this limitation.

At the bottom of the channel is the fader. I'll let you guess what this is for!

The other, non-channel, items include the master fader – actually a stereo fader underneath the single knob – and the record ready buttons and indicators. The transport controls are as you would expect on any tape machine. A couple of items missed out in this section will be mentioned as I progress.

Hook up

Figure 4.2 shows all the bits you need for a basic set up, and how they fit together. Notice that there are two main paths out of the unit: the master and the monitor paths, both of which come in left and right channels for stereo. The master outputs are connected to the stereo recorder, which may be DAT or reel-to-reel (best), or conventional stereo cassette (while you are saving up). The amount of signal – level – that comes out of the master outputs is vitally important for a noise-free and distortion-free recording, and is not related to the level that comes out of the monitor speakers. The monitor outputs are provided for you to listen to what's going on on the master, but you can set the level in the speakers to suit yourself rather than to suit what the tape requires in the track laying or mixing process. You can turn the monitor level up and down without affecting the signal to the tape in any way.

The other signal path out of the multitracker is the auxiliary send, or aux send for short. As you can see, this goes to a reverb unit, the two outputs from the reverb returning a stereo signal to the aux returns. There are two aux returns on any self-respecting multitracker, preferably with a level control –   probably a single stereo control rather than two mono ones. Some multitrackers don't have level controls on their aux returns. An uncontrolled aux return is sometimes called a 'bus in' input. The bus in, which has nothing to do with a Number 48 or a 90p fare, mixes directly with the master output to the stereo recorder. Therefore, to add reverb to your mix in the correct quantity, you need a reverb unit with an output level control. This is a point that needs to be checked when you are buying equipment, otherwise you will have to accept excessively noisy mixes with an uncontrolled reverb level output.

The great advantage of the multitracker is that it is so handy.

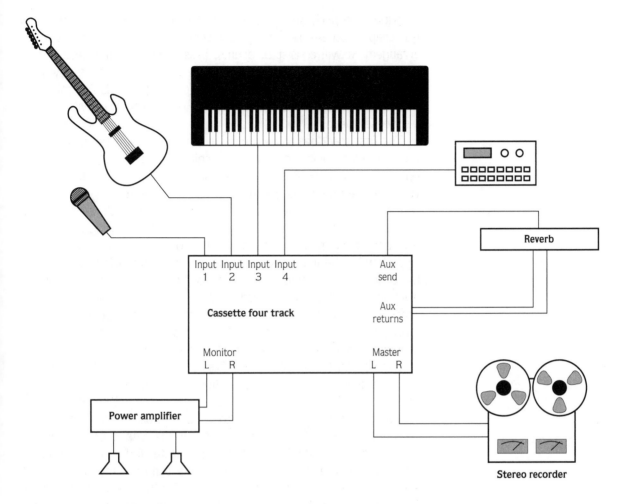

Notice how few cables there are in this system, and it can produce amazingly good results. Be prepared for a shock, cable-wise, when you upgrade.

Fig 4.2 Typical connections for a 4-track recording session

Track laying

Are you a live or a MIDI musician? There's no prejudice here because you can make good music either way on a multitracker. But let's concentrate on the guitar picking instrumentalist with a bit of vocal ability. We'll get him, or her, started by including a bass – guitar or synth – and a basic drum machine in the package.

Perhaps the most important factor in getting a good four track recording is the planning. Sometimes, you have to make an initial personal demo of a song in order to develop the arrangement. Then, with the instrumentation sorted out, you start again to make the definitive, properly planned, 'master' demo recording. Following my last chapter on simple arranging techniques, I shall assume that the arrangement will consist of drums, bass, chord backing, lead instrumental line and vocal. I'll add, just for fun, two vocal harmony lines. This adds up to seven different musical parts. It sounds like three too many for our poor little multitracker to cope with – but with a bit of a squeeze, it can.

The first track has to be the drum machine, simply because a musician can synchronise to a drum machine, but a drum machine can't sync to a musician. Besides the musical material in the drum track, you will need something extra – a count in. Without a count in, of course, you won't know when to come in. I find that the best count in is a quarter note hihat pulse lasting two bars, but missing out the last beat before the music comes in. We'll need that gap when we mix.

Following the instructions provided in your multitracker's manual, the drum machine should be routed to Track 1, the correct recording level set, and the track recorded. You could equally well start from Track 4 and work backwards. Don't start in the middle or you are more likely to run into feedback (a whistling tone at a high level) problems when we start bouncing (combining) tracks.

The second track will be our first overdub. This will probably be the bass line, but could be the chord backing. The drum track is recorded on Track 1 of the tape, so Channel 1 must be set to 'Tape' so you can hear it. The channel to which the bass is connected must be routed to Track 2. Since you want only the bass to be recorded on Track 2, only Channel 2's fader, and the master fader, must be raised. You can hear the drums on Track 1 by setting the monitor to 'Cue' and raising the cue level on that channel. Set the cue level on Channel 2 for a good working balance. The cue levels that you set do not affect the recording.

The procedure is repeated for the third track. Now you have only one track left, but four more parts to record. The thing to do is to bounce those three tracks onto Track 4. Bouncing is simply mixing a number of tracks onto another track on the same tape. Channels 1, 2 and 3 are routed to record onto Track 4 and are mixed together with the faders the way you will want to hear them in the final mix. Although you can have as many goes as you like at the bounce, once you are satisfied and proceed with the next stage, you are committed to what you have done. The next stage is to erase Tracks 1, 2 and 3! (Sometimes when you are bouncing tracks, you get a high pitched whistle as soon as you enter Record. This is due to feedback in the record head itself. It can usually be cured by simply lowering the recording level.)

With three tracks freed, you are ready for the next step. Since you have two harmony vocals to do, I would suggest recording these next onto Tracks 1 and 2, then bouncing them both to Track 3. The final stages would be recording the main vocal onto Track 1 and the lead instrumental line onto Track 2. Finished!

This is a fairly simple example. It is quite possible to record more than seven parts, in fact up to ten, without bouncing any track more than once. To do this, you need to add a live part each time you bounce. So when the drums, bass, and chords were bounced to Track 4, there might have been another part included at the same time. Also a third harmony vocal could have been added. It is slightly more difficult to add these extra parts because when you are recording parts individually it is possible to punch in, or drop in as it is sometimes called. All multitrackers these days have a socket for a punch in footswitch, with which you can play the tape and punch in and out of record mode at any time, correcting any wrong notes. When you are recording just one instrument, punching in is relatively easy. If several are being mixed together it is unlikely to work.

Working with MIDI expands the capabilities of the multitracker. Most sequencers will synchronise to tape. A sync pulse is recorded on Track 4 and thereafter the sequencer will sync to that. You only have three tracks to record music on, but you still have as many input channels as you had before, and sequenced instruments can supply other parts. More on this when I discuss multitrack and MIDI in Chapter 9.

Fig 4.3 Fostex XR5 – a simple but effective multitrack recorder

Mixing

Mixing is the part of the recording process where your raw tracks will turn into a finished master. It is a process that demands close attention to the sounds coming from the speakers and painstaking adjustment and readjustment, even with just four tracks.

The first stage of mixing consists of listening to the individual tracks, some of which will contain more than one instrument. What I like to listen for in the individual tracks is the character of the track, to find out what its essential components are, and see what qualities it has that are not really required. Even with just four tracks, it is easy to get a mix that sounds like all the instruments are fighting with other for their share of the space between the stereo speakers. What we really want is to get them all working together, each making a valuable contribution to the whole sound.

To optimise each track, I experiment with the EQ. I consider whether a sound benefits by having a particular frequency range boosted. If it does, I do just that, and just enough to make a difference. If it doesn't, then I try cutting that frequency range. If, for example, the instrument doesn't make any useful contribution in the high frequency range, then turn down the high EQ and reduce any HF clutter it is producing. Another example: the bass instrument is producing the bass frequencies. Other bass-heavy instruments are probably congesting the bottom end, so lighten them up.

After experimenting with EQ on the individual tracks and when you have decided where to pan the tracks in the stereo picture, see how much reverb each track needs just by itself. At this stage, add no more than makes a difference. This individual approach will help tune in the ear to the capabilities of each track and what they may be able to do for the mix when you raise all the faders together. From this point on, it's up to you. You are the only person who can tell what adjustments improve the mix, and what makes it less good. How long will it take you to arrive at the perfect mix, and be ready to transfer it to stereo tape? Even with just four channels and a reverb unit, don't be surprised if it takes a couple of hours. When you move up to more tracks, it may take longer still.

Assuming the mix is right, you have all your fader levels set and have planned any level changes you want to make (not forgetting to set the level on your stereo recorder), take out a Chinagraph pencil and make a mark next to the centre of the fader knob on each channel. Remember that hihat count in? Play the tape up to the seventh beat and pause, so that when you start, you miss out any of the extraneous sounds that accumulate before the beginning of the music (if you have a reel-to-reel stereo recorder, then you will be able to edit them out rather than doing it this way). Set the stereo recorder to record, and hit the play button on the multitracker. As the final notes die away, pull down the channel faders first, and the master fader as the reverb dies away. This ensures that your master ends in silence rather than noise and hiss. The Chinagraph marks are for when you make a hash of it and want to do it again. Just reset the faders to the marks and have another go.

Hopefully, this chapter will have explained just a few of the techniques of multitrack recording in a simple way. But there's a lot more to it than can be covered in a couple of pages. Later on we shall see how multitrack recordings are made on a grander scale.

Tascam 564 Minidisc Portastudio

The mixing console

One of my favourite mixing consoles is the Audio Developments Picomixer. It has six inputs, two outputs, and is about the size of a briefcase, if somewhat on the chubby side. It is small, but it is not cheap – it costs around £2000, depending on the options you have ordered. Does this sound like a lot of money for a six channel mixer? Well, £2000 is by most standards a lot of money, but what you get is a very professional, robust little unit which is precisely suited to its intended function, location recording. If you don't need more than six mics, but you do need good quality sound and the feeling of confidence that you will never be let down, then the Picomixer is just the thing to have.

The point that I am working up to is that to many people the words 'mixing console' are pretty well synonymous with 'large' and 'complicated'. A mixer does not in fact have to be either of these. It has to be able to do a job of work. This job may demand a lot of facilities, or it may demand a smaller number which are exactly appropriate to the task in hand. What I intend to look at here is a typical recording console and see what facilities it has, and to show at each stage how they fit in with other items of studio equipment and with the recording process as a whole.

Mix bus

'It's very impressive, but what does it actually do?', asked the A&R man about the mixing console, in an unguarded moment.

The recording process basically consists of taking sounds from a variety of sources, modifying the character of those sounds if necessary, mixing them together in a subjectively pleasing way and storing them on a permanent medium – usually tape. The mixing console is the control centre for all of these processes. In fact, virtually every signal flowing from one piece of equipment to another in the studio will flow through the console. Figure 5.1 shows the typical selection of sources and destinations.

Inside the console, the signals do not simply pass from input to output. The essential component of the mixing console is the mix bus. The phrase 'mix bus' derives, just like 'London bus', from the Latin word 'omnibus' meaning 'for all'. In fact if you think of how a motor

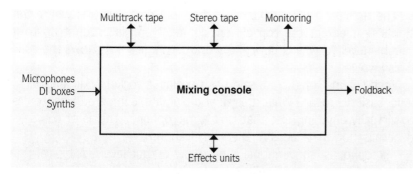

Fig 5.1 Sources and destinations of a mixing console

bus operates you will not be far from the mix bus concept: a bus travels along a fixed route from suburban point A to city centre B. In the suburban areas, it picks up passengers from various points along the route. When it reaches the city centre, they all get off and go to work. The mix bus plies a route as well, from the left hand end of the console to the right. It starts by picking up various signals from the inputs and takes them to a destination, which will be one of the outputs from the console. In the console, there is only one suburban area (the input section) and all buses pass through it. There will be several outputs and each bus goes to one output only. Figure 5.2 shows the signals from four channels flowing into one bus.

The basic console has a number of inputs, known as channels, and outputs, known as groups. A console with twelve channels mixing into two groups would be fine as a PA console. Twelve mics could connect to the channel inputs and the two group outputs could go to left and right loudspeakers via a stereo power amp. A recording console needs two extra sections: the monitor section, which enables you to hear the output of the multitrack tape recorder, and a master section which – among other things – has a switch which lets you hear the main stereo output of the console or alternatively routes the output of the stereo tape recorder directly to the monitor amp and speakers. Figure 5.3 shows where to look for these sections on a typical console. This orientation of facilities is known as the split monitoring design. The alternative is called in-line, in which the monitor section is combined into the channels. I am going to stick to the split system for the moment because it is easier to explain, and perhaps a little bit more logical.

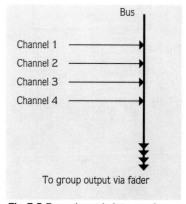

Fig 5.2 Four channels into one bus

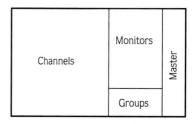

Fig 5.3 Layout of typical console

The channel

The channel is where the input signal is conditioned so that it is suitable for further processing in the console; it provides equalisation to change the character of the signal; finally it routes the signal to one or more buses and controls its level. Let's take a stage by stage look...

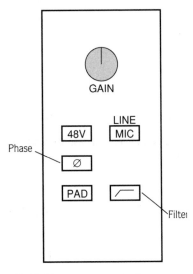

Fig 5.4 Input stage controls

The first part of the channel is the input stage. This is where the signal first enters the console environment and is brought up to a suitable level for the circuitry to work on. Figure 5.4 shows the controls involved.

Each channel of the console has two input sockets, Mic and Line. 'Mic' basically means what it says, you plug a mic in here. 'Line' refers to virtually anything else that isn't a microphone. This is of course a generalisation that needs further clarification:

Microphones, conventionally, have low output levels. A typical figure would be around 10 millivolts (one hundredth of a volt). The console likes to work on a signal level of around one volt to keep well above the inevitable noise voltages that will be present in the circuitry. This means that the signal from the mic has to be boosted by 100 times, or 40dB (a gain of 40dB means exactly the same as 'multiply the voltage by 100'). Of course, when I say that 10mV comes out of a microphone, that depends on the level of the sound source, its distance from the mic, and also depends on how the sound level varies. In practice, a mic input needs to have a range of gain from 20dB (10x) up to 60dB (1000x). A desirable range is from 0dB (no gain at all – the signal stays the same) to 80dB (10,000x). This would cover all situations from the mic being placed inside a bass drum to a watch ticking at twenty paces.

There would be no advantage in providing more than 80dB gain for even quieter sounds because the noise produced by the mic would be amplified above the console's noise level. The mic input here has a switchable 48 volt phantom power supply.

Pretty well any equipment that is connected to the mains produces a line level output, or near enough, so this is connected to the line input. Ideally, the gain control should still operate when the channel is switched to line input. On some consoles, variable line gain is dispensed with as a cost-cutting, inconvenience-causing measure. A good range of line gain would be, if you can get it, from -20dB (which would actually reduce the signal level by a factor of 10) to +20dB. (One reason why you might like to reduce the signal level is when you want to use only a small amount of the signal on that channel in the mix. If you can reduce the input gain, the fader can be operated at a higher, more convenient, level).

Not everything that produces a signal can be connected to the mic or line inputs. To reduce noise levels, these inputs are normally designed to be fairly low impedance – jargon meaning that the inputs need to see a lot of electrons coming down the cable. Some signal sources just cannot produce a lot of electrons, or a lot of current which amounts to the same thing. The most typical example is the electric guitar. Although a guitar may put out a healthy voltage, it

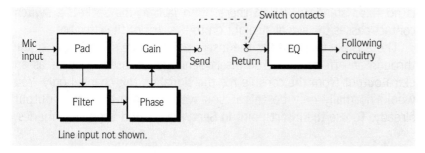

Line input not shown.

Fig 5.5 Arrangement of pad, filter, phase and gain switches

hasn't got the 'oomph' to drive a mixer input directly. In this case a device called a DI – Direct Injection – box is used between the guitar and console.

The other switches in the diagram are the pad, filter and phase switches. The pad, in a properly designed console, will cut the level of an input signal by 20dB before it reaches any active device in the circuitry. This is so that if you have a really high level input signal, it can be cut down to size before it has chance to produce any distortion. If a console has a switched gain control, as opposed to one with a continuous travel, the pad may be invisibly incorporated on one of the wafers – sections – of the switch.

In theory, the filter ought to be an adjunct to the pad. As you know, directional microphones produce high levels of low frequency signal when they are used close to the sound source. The filter, if it comes before any active circuit component such as a transistor or integrated circuit, can deal with these low frequencies. Often the pad and filter come after some of the active circuit elements in which case they don't work as protection against distortion, they are just accessory level and EQ controls. Figure 5.5 shows the preferred internal arrangement.

Figure 5.6 shows the effect of the phase switch. It simply turns the signal upside down. This is useful when one of your microphones, or one of your cables, is wired in reverse – pins 2 and 3 of the XLR connector being swapped. This happens more often than you would imagine and produces horrible frequency cancellation effects. Also, where several mics are being used close together, there may be random phase effects even when they are all wired correctly. It is sometimes helpful to experiment with the phase buttons to see whether the sound improves subjectively. Going back to Figure 5.5, you will notice the insert point. The insert point is typically used for connecting a compressor or noise gate. A unit connected here will operate only on this one channel. The insert point on many consoles is in the form of a stereo jack socket, the tip connection being the insert send and the ring connection being the insert return. You will not be surprised to learn that some consoles have it the other way round, there

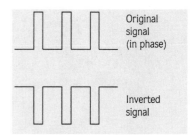

Original signal (in phase)

Inverted signal

Fig 5.6 Effect of phase switch

is no fixed standard. When there is no jack in the socket, a switch contact passes the signal straight on to the rest of the circuitry.

There is another use for the insert point beside sending the signal through an effects unit. The insert send can be used by itself as an extra output from the console for the signal on this channel only. You would normally only do this if you were using every other output already. To use the insert point in Send/Return and Send Only modes,

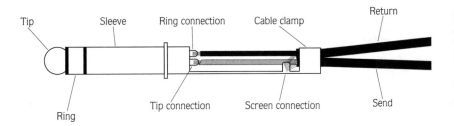

Fig 5.7 Send/return connections

as I shall call them, you need two different types of cable. The first is shown in Figure 5.7. Notice how two cables must be forced into one jack plug for Send/Return operation.

For Send Only, you need to link the tip and ring of the jack with a piece of wire so that the signal passes through the insert as normal (Figure 5.8). Remember that when you plug a jack into the socket, the internal connection is temporarily broken away.

Sometimes the insert point is positioned directly after the input circuitry. This is great for noise gating because once you have set the gain, the gating threshold doesn't vary. Other consoles place the

Fig 5.8 Send only connections

insert point after the EQ. This is subjectively better for compression, but it makes gating difficult because you have to adjust the gate each time you change the EQ. Some consoles let you have it both ways (at a price!).

EQ

After the input circuitry, the signal is big enough and strong enough to be sent to the rest of the console. Its first test of manhood will be the EQ section. EQ stands for equalisation. It is very strange terminology because we are not making anything equal to anything else. The word originates from telephone systems and we seem to be stuck with it, at least until someone comes up with something better. The EQ section of the channel is a glorified tone control. It changes the frequency balance of the signal, boosting the highs, cutting the lows, sucking out the middle, adding a presence peak... but let's cut the jargon. Let's look at a typical console EQ section, as in Figure 5.9.

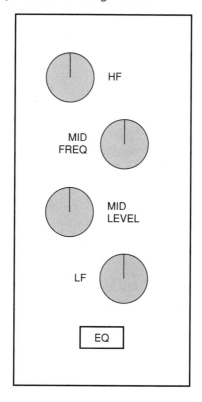

Fig 5.9 Three band EQ section

This is a three band EQ section. The HF control cuts or boosts the level of the signal above a set frequency. The LF control similarly cuts or boosts the level below a set frequency. The Mid section has two controls, one which sets the amount of cut or boost, one which selects the frequency at which this takes place. One possible point of confusion for the newcomer to mixing console operation is the fact that if the Mid Level control is set to its centre position, the Mid Frequency control will have no effect on the sound. This of course is entirely logical when you think about it.

An essential feature of any EQ section is the In/Out switch. This has two functions. The minor function is so that if you are not using any EQ on that channel, the extra circuitry can be switched out of the signal path since it all adds extra noise. The major function of the EQ In/Out switch is so that the engineer can assess the difference between the EQ'd and unEQ'd – flat – signal. It really is very important to know that you are actually improving the sound as you twid-

Fig 5.10 More complex EQ section

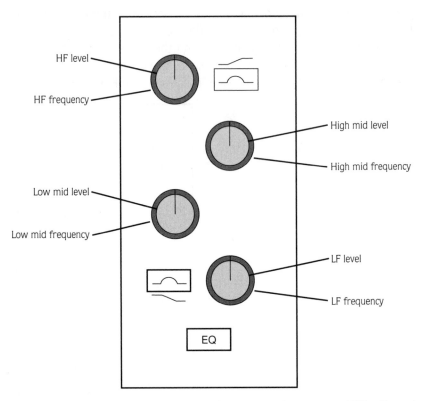

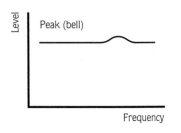

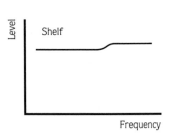

Fig 5.11 Peaking response and shelving response

dle the knobs. Without the switch, comparisons are difficult and rarely made.

The EQ described above is really pretty rudimentary, although surprisingly few consoles go further than this. Higher up in the console price range you get an EQ that can really do things to the sound. It will look rather like Figure 5.10.

Some console EQs get more complex even than this. The real advantage of this EQ is in the switched frequency HF and LF controls. Fixed frequency controls may or may not operate on the correct part of the audio spectrum for the instrument you are recording, probably not as is usually the case. With switched EQ frequencies, you can home in. The switches close to the HF and LF sections are the peak/shelf switches.

Figure 5.11 shows the difference between the two. A peaking response boosts – or cuts – a particular band of frequencies around a centre frequency. The shelving response boosts all frequencies above – in the case of HF – a set frequency. These two responses offer distinctly different sounds. The shelf response is particularly good when the slope of the curve where the response changes is fairly steep.

Auxiliary sends

Following the signal path further down the channel strip we find the auxiliary send controls. These are extra signal paths out of the console, separate from the main outputs. Figure 5.12 shows what the typical aux send section will look like. Figure 5.13 is the internal view on what's happening. But why do we need auxiliary sends? What can they do that can't be achieved with the normal group outputs?

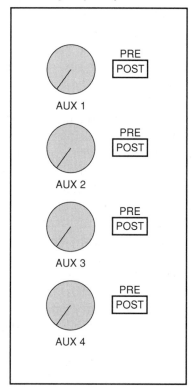

Fig 5.12 Auxiliary sends. The switches follow the convention where the legend on the button shows what happens when the switch is pressed in. The legend above the button shows the situation when the switch is left out

Each auxiliary on a console is like a separate mixer, independent of the main mix set up on the channel faders. Whatever the position of the faders, a completely different balance of sounds can emerge from each of the auxiliary outputs. So a mixer with 4 auxiliaries can provide five completely different mixes of the same sound sources. Four auxes, by the way, is a good number for a small console, eight is better and more versatile for a larger model. PA engineers probably wouldn't be satisfied with twenty, but that's a different story.

The first and foremost use for auxiliary sends in a music recording studio is for foldback. A group of musicians in the studio will want to be able to hear themselves and each other very clearly as they play. They will also need to hear any tracks already recorded on tape, and perhaps a click track. For this they will need a set of headphones each. The foldback is simply the signal supplied to these headphones. Auxiliary 1 can be used as the foldback send on each channel. (In fact, sometimes an auxiliary is actually labelled 'Foldback'. It is still just an ordinary aux and can be used for other purposes). The guitar, bass, drums, keyboards and whatever are mixed using the Aux 1 controls to provide a musically balanced signal completely independent of the levels of the signals going to the multitrack recorder. The balance between the instruments in the foldback is purely for the musicians' benefit since it will not affect what is recorded on tape. It's up to the musicians to decide amongst themselves how loud to have each instrument in their headphones. The overall level in the phones is determined by the aux master control.

Musicians, as any engineer will know, are never satisfied with the foldback balance. So far, I have assumed that one aux send will provide a foldback signal for everyone concerned. But it is more than likely that each musician will have his or her own preferences and two or more auxes will have to be used to provide different foldback mixes (requiring a different headphone amplifier for each mix of course). The one thing that must not happen with foldback mixes, once they are set to the musicians' requirements, is for the levels of the instruments to change. You may, for the purposes of the recording, want to adjust fader levels as the players become more enthusiastic and confident in their parts, to set the correct level going to tape. This means that the aux sends used for foldback must be pre fade. In other words, the signal is taken from the channel from a point in the circuitry before the fader. On pre fade, the setting of the fader has no effect on the level of the signal going to the aux output. The signal routing for pre fade can be traced in Figure 5.13.

The other major use of aux sends is for effects, principally reverb. If Aux Sends 1 and 2 are being used for two foldback mixes, Aux Send 3 will very probably be patched into the reverb unit, although

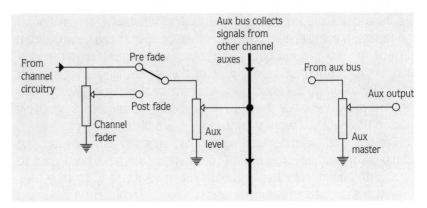

Fig 5.13 Auxiliary circuitry

you can of course use any aux for any purpose. Particularly during mixdown, a separate balance of signals is sent to the reverb unit using the aux send. This time the level coming from each channel to the reverb should be controlled by the fader, as well as by the aux send control. Usually, if you fade a channel down you want its reverb to die away too. This is done using the post fade setting on the auxiliary. The signal is now taken from a point after the fader so there are now two positions in the channel module – the aux level control and the fader - where the level of the aux send is determined.

This is also shown on Figure 5.13 The best consoles have a Pre/Post switch for each aux, so you can combine pre fade and post fade sends any way you like. To cut costs however, many consoles have one switch per pair of auxes which is a bit of nuisance. The aux master, one of which is provided for each aux send, is the master level control for each aux bus. If you want to change the overall level of the signal going to the foldback or reverb, adjust the aux master. If one channel needs tweaking, use the individual aux control on the channel.

Fader

'Hang on a minute, he's missed a bit!', says the eagle eyed reader. Well, yes I have. I've postponed the pan and routing section which is positioned above the fader until a bit later. For the moment, I'm sticking within the channel module before describing how it slots in with everything else. And when you come to think about it, the fader is the next step in the signal chain anyway. The signal doubles back, physically if not electronically, before hopping on the mix bus.

The fader simply controls the level of the signal in the channel and that's it - almost. Among all the controls on the console, the fader is the only one that you operate in a straight line. The simple reason for this is because you can see at a glance the relative levels of all the channels. Mixing with rotary controls would be a pain. Before linear faders were invented there were things called quadrant faders where the knob moved in a circular path – a vertically orientated circle – over electrical stud contacts. Apparently these are still popular with some engineers who work to picture because they can feel where they are without having to look at them.

The fader has the job of controlling the level of the signal between minus infinity decibels and +10dB. No fader yet made can reduce the signal level completely to zero even at its lowest setting. Expensive consoles have micro-switches built in to the fader so that when it is brought all the way down, the signal is physically switched off. Figure 5.14 shows how a fader works electrically. The signal comes in at the

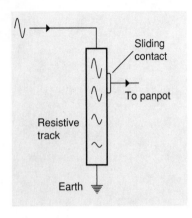

Fig 5.14 Fader internals

at the top of the resistive track and makes its way towards earth – zero volts. All the way down the track the available level of the signal reduces. (It is actually amplified by 10dB before the fader. That's the way the fader allows you to boost the level, even though the mechanical part of it can only reduce it). The sliding contact on the fader picks off the signal at a point along the track, the position will determine the signal level. It's probably a good idea to point out here that faders are very sensitive to dirt. It's important that fades are smooth and click free. If the sliding contact has to climb over a lump of cigarette ash then it probably won't be. Keep the ashtray, and your can of Coke, well away. When you are cleaning the console, brush the dust away from the fader slots, not into them.

Solo

Just above the fader there will be a solo or PFL button. PFL stands for Pre Fade Listen and is sometimes verbalised as 'piffle' by jargon mongers in the trade. There are several ways in which this button can operate. Sometimes a console offers just one, possibly wrongly labelled, way. High end consoles may have options. PFL – Pre Fade Listen – is the simplest system. If the button above the fader is labelled PFL, then pressing it will allow you to listen to that channel alone on the monitor speakers at a fixed level unaffected by the fader. You may press the PFLs on several channels simultaneously if you wish, but they will all be mixed at their top-of-the-fader levels.

Solo is where you hear the channel with its fader setting intact. This is sometimes known as AFL – After Fade Listen (or 'affle').

Solo in place (or cut solo or kill solo) is an interesting concept. PFL and AFL work by switching the channel's signal from the mix bus to a separate solo bus, the monitor output being switched to this bus also. SIP doesn't use an extra bus. If you press the button on Channel 1, all the other channels will be muted, thus allowing you to hear Channel 1 only. If you are mixing when you press this type of solo button, then you wreck the mix. (It would be worse still if you were broadcasting!). The other types of solo are non-destructive. The advantage of SIP is that there should also be a solo safe button on each channel. If you press this on all your effects returns, then soloing any channel will give you that channel in its correct place in the stereo image and with its reverb and other effects intact. Solo in place may not be usable in all circumstances, but it is very powerful when used with care. I wish more consoles offered it.

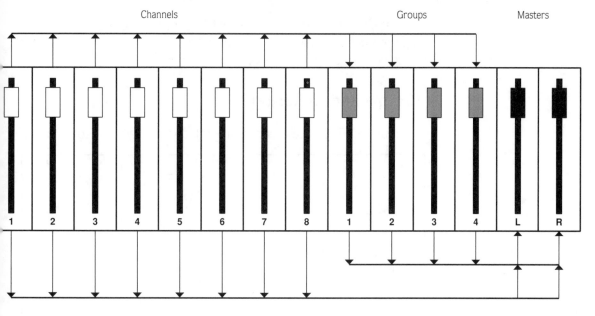

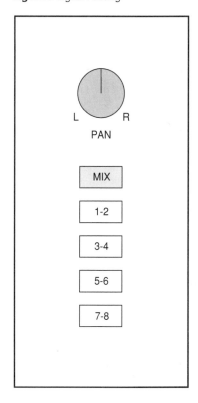

Channels   Groups   Masters

1 2 3 4 5 6 7 8   1 2 3 4   L R

Fig 5.15 Signal flow between channels, groups (subgroups), and masters

Fig 5.16 Signal routing

Routing

It's time now for the signal to emerge from the narrow confines of the channel module. But where should it go? These days, most medium size consoles have a number of channels, eight or sixteen groups and a stereo master (or mix) output. The signal flow is shown in Figure 5.15.

As you can see, you can route the signal from the channel directly to a group and/or to the master, or to a group and then from the group to the master. When going from channel-to-group-to-master, the group is usually called a subgroup. It hasn't actually changed physically but it uses the technique known as 'subgrouping', so when I refer to groups and subgroups I am talking about the same thing, but operated differently.

The routing section of the typical console will look rather like that in Figure 5.16. Notice the arrangement of buttons: MIX, 1-2, 3-4, 5-6, 7-8. 'Mix' will be used, obviously, when mixing down to stereo. It is also used for monitoring because in many consoles, the mix bus and the monitor bus – both stereo buses – are one and the same. '1-2' means that the signal passes through the pan pot – short for 'panoramic potentiometer' – before passing to Bus 1 and Bus 2. The pan pot is rotated to the left to send the signal to Group 1, to the right to send it to Group 2. If the control is positioned in the centre, then it goes to both buses. All the routing buttons work in this way.

PAN

MIX

1-2

3-4

5-6

7-8

A step up from this arrangement is the one where each bus has a separate button. This gives greater flexibility and better crosstalk and noise performance. Of course, it costs more.

Groups and metering

In Figure 5.17, you can see the group faders and associated subgroup

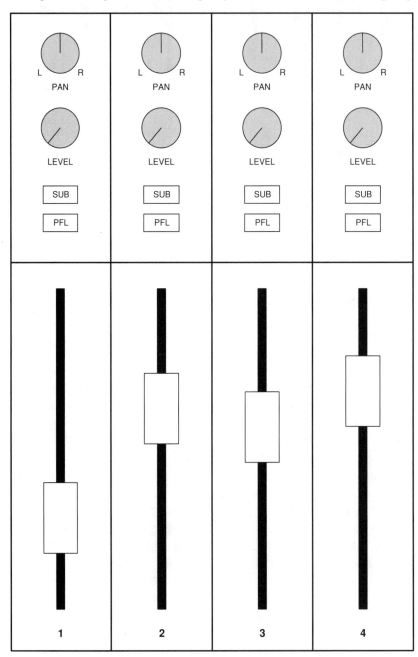

Fig 5.17 Group faders and sub-group controls

paraphernalia. As I mentioned earlier, it's a matter of usage. One would talk about a 'group' when the signal is leaving the console directly after the fader, a 'subgroup' when it is going on somewhere else before emerging from a different output. Groups only have faders, and perhaps solo buttons. They are used simply to control the level of a mixed group of channels (see where the name comes from?). To use the groups as subgroups and mix them into the masters you need, obviously, to press the 'Subgroup' button. The level and pan controls will now act on the post fader output of the group, as in Figure 5.18.

You would use subgroups like this if you had a large number of mics on a drum kit which you had carefully balanced. If you mixed these into stereo to a pair of subgroups, then you could adjust the level of the kit as a whole with just two faders, rather than having painstakingly to adjust each individual channel fader. More on this topic later.

The output from the groups is the point where you must look at the level of the signal. Too much level going to the multitrack will result in distortion, too little will mean excess noise, so effective metering is necessary. There are three sorts of meters in common use on mixing consoles: VU, PPM and LED bargraph. The one thing these all have in common is that they should preferably be in alignment with the meters on the multitrack tape recorder. If this is so, you need never look at the meters on the multitrack, just at those close at hand on the console – your workstation if you like.

VU meter

The letters 'VU' stand for 'Volume Units'. VUs have been around for decades and show the average level of the signal. This is rather a pity because it's the peak level of the signal which we need to keep a close eye on to avoid distorting the tape. Impulsive sounds like drums will give a very low average reading compared to their true peak levels.

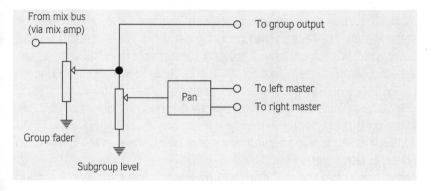

Fig 5.18 Subgroup circuitry

You need to interpret the readings VU meters give for satisfactory results. Because of the uncertainty involved, VU meters have been dubbed 'Virtually Useless'! Like looking through frosted glass, you can see that something is happening but you are not sure quite what!

PPM meter

PPM stands for Peak Programme Meter. These, as you might guess, give true peak readings. They have fast moving needles which are powered up their scales by special driver circuitry. PPMs are very good, and very easy on the eye too. But they cost a lot so we need an alternative:

LED bargraph

The LED bargraph, with PPM characteristics, is almost standard these days on low and mid price equipment. The more the equipment costs, the more LED segments you get in each column, and therefore the more accurate the resolution. Top notch consoles are treated to bargraphs that are probably more expensive than the PPMs they replace. These are for engineers who can't afford to take chances.

Master

The Master section of the console has two faders – left and right – and all the extra twiddly bits that a good console, in fact any console, needs. The left and right master outputs obviously go to the stereo tape recorder. The monitor outputs go to the power amp and speakers so you can hear what's going on. Figure 5.19 shows those extra bits and pieces:

Mix/tape switch: This lets you hear the stereo output of the console or the output of the stereo tape recorder through the monitor speakers.

Talkback allows you to speak to the musicians in the studio, perhaps through a separate output from the console or maybe through the auxiliary outputs used for foldback.

Slate lets you make an announcement on the tape, multitrack or stereo, such as 'Take 32, introduction – yet again'. Often the slate facility records a very low frequency tone on the tape as well as the speech. When you are fast winding the tape, this tone can be heard raised in pitch. This helps you find your way between takes.

Oscillator: This is for putting reference tones on your master tape. More on this in Chapter 14.

Monitor level, studio monitor level and *headphone level* I think need no explanation.

Dim turns down the monitor level by a set amount, probably around 30dB. It is best always to monitor at the same level for the sake of

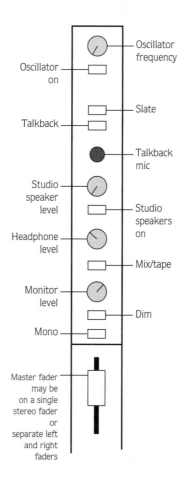

Oscillator frequency

Oscillator on

Slate

Talkback

Talkback mic

Studio speaker level

Studio speakers on

Headphone level

Mix/tape

Monitor level

Dim

Mono

Master fader may be on a single stereo fader or separate left and right faders

Fig 5.19 Master section controls

consistency during the session. The Dim button makes it easy to cut the level by 30dB when you need a quick consultation, then reset to exactly the level you had before.

Monitor mixing

The final section of the console is the monitor section. In the split monitor style of console this is a section to itself to the right of the channels, probably above the group faders. In an in line console, the monitor controls are in the channel modules.

This is less easy to explain, but let's say for now that they achieve much the same thing – they enable you to listen to the tracks you have already recorded on the multitrack while overdubbing, and also let you make a rough mix as you progress.

A typical monitor section is shown in Figure 5.20. As you can see, it is a mixer in its own right with level, pan and aux sends. The aux

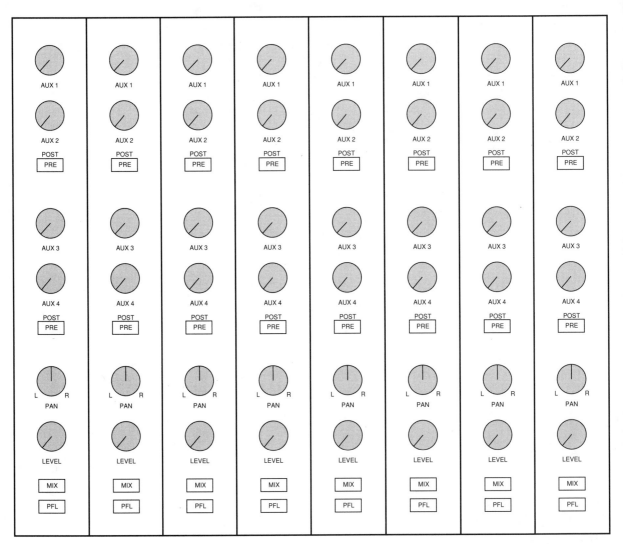

Fig 5.20 Monitor section controls

sends are there so that you can send the signals from the multitrack to the foldback, and also apply reverb if you fancy it.

The outputs from the monitor mixer go to the main stereo mix bus which means that you can use these monitor inputs as extra signal inputs if you wish. Just the job for those additional MIDI-synced synths and samplers.

The mixing console has probably the steepest learning curve of any item of studio equipment. It has so many functions and so many possibilities, and let's face it, so many knobs and switches that it is bound to take some time to come to terms with. The good news is that once you know one console thoroughly, it's a lot easier to learn your second, easier still the third. They are all slightly different, but in any one sound engineering field – studio, PA, theatre etc – the functions have to be similar because the various makes of console all have a similar job to do.

Now that I have covered some of the mixing console basics, it's time to start looking at how it is used in practice. In the next chapter, I shall be examining the procedures and techniques involved in running a recording session with several musicians and acoustic and electric instruments – a band in other words. This is where the fun really starts!

The patchbay

In any studio where there is a mixing console (that's every studio!), there will probably also be a patchbay. The patchbay is simply a collection of sockets, all on one panel, which are connected to all the inputs and outputs of each and every piece of equipment in the room.

Standard patchcords can be used to link them together. The connections between the equipment that are necessary for normal studio operations will almost certainly have been made using switch contacts behind the patchbay's front panel during installation. The 'normals' on the patchbay are those connections which are made during installation. These use the switched contacts on the jack sockets which open when you insert a patchcord into an input. Thus you can reconfigure the studio's standard set up in a matter of seconds or minutes.

Learning the patchbay

In a commercial studio, one of the first things any engineer will advise a new studio junior to do is to 'learn the patchbay'. When you have learned the patchbay, you will know how the equipment in the studio is connected, and you will also know how to connect any piece of equipment to any other.

For instance, you may want to compress a vocal. To do this you will need to patch a compressor into the insert points of the appropriate mixer channel. If you want to add reverb to a mix, you will have to make sure that one of the console's auxiliary outputs is connected to the input of the reverb unit, and that the outputs of the reverb are connected back to the console's auxiliary returns, or to a pair of channels.

Figure 5.21 shows a small patchbay. Notice that rows of outputs alternate with rows of inputs. Each output is normalled to the input directly below except in the case of the compressors and noise gates, so you can tell virtually at a glance what the connections are. (Compressors, gates and little used effects units are not usually normalled.)

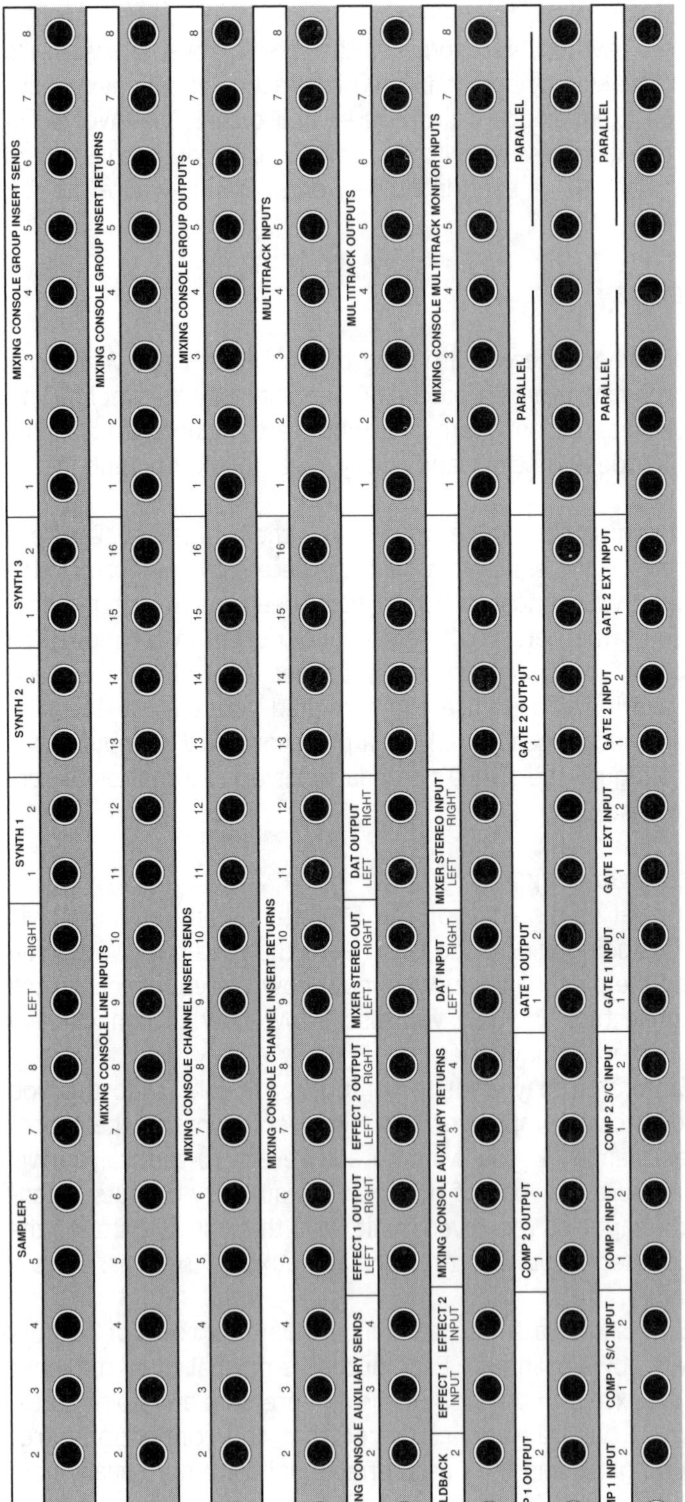

Fig 5.21 A small patchbay

Study this sample layout until you feel you understand how the equipment in the studio interacts. When you come to study the patchbay in a real studio you will find that things have probably shifted around a bit, but the overall pattern will be basically the same. The parallels are, by the way, simply sets of sockets wired together so that you can patch one output into more than one input.

The session

Recording a band in a studio can be a lot of fun, but it will test your abilities over a pretty wide range. Do you, for instance, have the diplomatic skills of a Secretary General of the United Nations; the sleight of hand of a member of the Magic Circle; the persuasiveness of a door to door life insurance salesman; the mind reading capability of an electroencephalograph? Well, if you can boast all these skills and more, don't forget that you have to be a recording engineer too! Recording a band means dealing with people, and people can be a lot more awkward and demanding than machines such as samplers and sequencers, but the end result can amply justify the effort put in.

As I said earlier, I am going to consider the typical situation where the engineer works directly with the musicians, without the assistance of a producer. Taking the whole spectrum of recording studios into account, from garage level up, this probably applies to the majority. Also, in situations where one of the musicians considers himself to be the producer of the recording, the fact is that the engineer is probably doing most of the real production work, even if he or she doesn't claim a fair share of the credit! I'm going to look at the recording process mainly from the engineer's point of view, but if you are principally a musician working on the other side of the window then perhaps you'll get an idea of what it's like for the guy, or gal, in the hot seat and hopefully end up with better studio recordings.

Preparation

This is where the bit about mind reading comes in. From my own experience, a request like, "I just want a straight cassette copy", actually means "I'd like you to cut out eight bars from the middle, get rid of some of the hiss, speed it up slightly – and can you make another couple of copies while you're at it". If someone says, "It's just a basic track with a vocal and a couple of guitar overdubs", what they mean is, "It's a basic track with a lead vocal, three harmony vocals, several guitar overdubs through a stereo effects unit, and I wouldn't mind a few tracks of that synth you have over there".

It's not as though things always escalate completely out of proportion, but when you budget for a certain amount of time or a certain number of tracks, you can count on having to add on a fair safety margin, and if that margin isn't there it's the engineer that's going to get the blame. The answer is to talk the project through thoroughly before even opening the instrument cases. Unless the band is experienced in studio work, you will really have to pump out the information you need otherwise you are going to have problems later on. Here are a few sample questions that will set the ball rolling:

Have you played this song live before?
If the song has been part of the band's set for months, then they'll know how it goes and will probably have a good idea of the studio embellishments they would like to add. If it's a new song then you are virtually bound to find sections where the musicians are not sufficiently confident, or indeed sections which just don't sound right under analytical studio conditions. The advantage of recording a song which hasn't been played live too much is that the musicians will be more open to suggestions on how the arrangement could be changed for the benefit of the recording. Performing arrangements and recording arrangements should ideally be worked out separately according to their respective needs.

What is the instrumentation of the song?
Rather than just counting the instruments, you need to know whether the guitarist, and possibly the bassist, use any effects pedals, or if there are any surprises in store that ought to come out now rather than later.

What does the vocal arrangement consist of?
You need to know how many vocal parts to expect, and also establish as soon as possible who the lead vocalist is so that you can start building up the friendly relationship that you'll need later on.

What do you intend adding to the arrangement that you don't play live?
Make sure you have had a full answer from the keyboard player before you leave this topic, they are notorious for wanting to add endless embellishments. It's not a problem if you know about them now.

Is there anything else you think I should know?
Don't expect a response to this question, but at least the ball is in the band's court and they can't come back later and say, "Well you didn't ask about..."

Perhaps this is starting to sound like a battle of wits between the band and the engineer when really it ought to be a total collaboration towards getting a good recording of a good song. Such a total collaboration however only comes when you have a good communicative relationship with the members of the band individually, where they respect the engineer's advice and ideas, and where the engineer understands the musicians' aims and needs. But all this takes time (and is rarely properly achieved even within the band itself). The question and answer routine, properly applied, is an invaluable short-cut. At this stage, you should have a good idea of how the recording will proceed, and you will know whether you have enough tracks for all the instrumental and vocal parts or whether you will have to bounce some tracks together. You will also be able to plan the sequence of overdubs, and think about when those difficult — but important - vocals should be recorded.

Setting up

Now it's time for the band to unpack their instruments and for the engineer to decide how he is going to tackle them. Note that he is not going to help the band unpack, he will be directing them to where he wants them in the studio, and taking mental notes of the equipment coming out from the flight cases. A good layout for the band in the studio is important, but fairly easily achieved if you have enough space. The two essential points are that the members of the band must face each other and that microphones, as far as practicable, must only pick up the instrument or amp at which they are pointed. Figure 6.1 shows a typical layout which should be fairly self explanatory. Notice that the bassist stands next to the drummer, this is always the case and helps towards greater precision in the rhythm section. Although the layout of the band is the engineer's responsibility, he should of course consult the band just in case there is some special requirement.

When all the instruments and amps are set up, adjusted and ready to go, send everyone except the drummer to the pub for an hour (the singer especially will want to lubricate his vocal cords). Unless you have worked with the band before it will take a good while to mic up the kit and get a basic drum sound. If you have the other band members around during this time they will clutter up the studio and control room, make noises with their instruments and generally get in your hair at a time when you want to concentrate on the most difficult instrument engineers ever have to cope with. If there are no problems with the kit itself, an hour or so should be enough to get a good basic drum sound, which fits in with the time scale allowed for demo recordings. Of course, it is quite possible to spend much more time than this getting as close to perfection as you can. And exactly how do you get close to perfection in drum recording? Well, you'll have to wait until Chapter 7 for that!

Let's assume that you have your drum mics set up and you're ready to start on the other instruments – guitar, bass and keyboards. The guitarist will almost certainly want to play through an amplifier, hopefully a small one that doesn't have to be turned all the way up to

Fig 6.1 Possible studio layout for four piece rock band

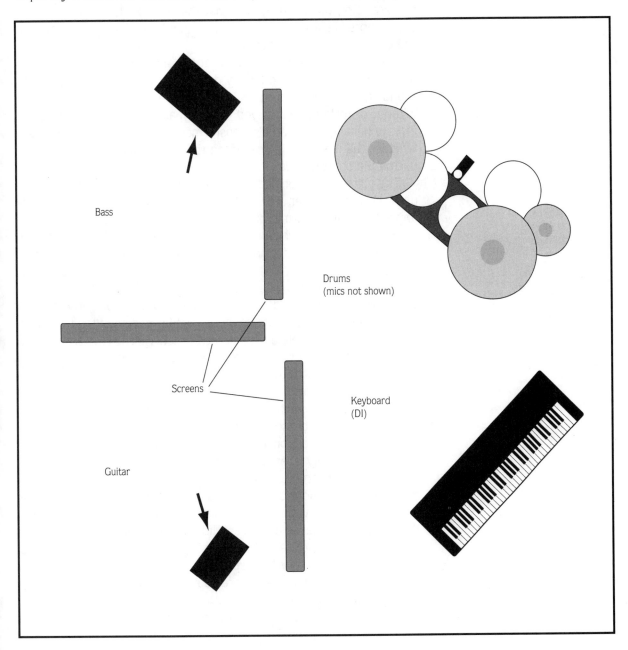

a hundred watts' worth of neighbour-blasting power to sound good. In Figure 6.2 the guitarist's amp is shown with a mic pointing at the edge of the speaker (I shall use the convention of representing microphones by appropriately directed arrows). It may come as a surprise the first time you experiment with mic positioning on a guitar amp that a wide variety of different sound qualities can be obtained by mic placement and pointing. The centre of any speaker normally produces the brightest, cleanest and punchiest sound. This may be the sound you are after, but I usually find that the edge of the speaker gives a sound more like actually hearing the amp with the naked ear – from a rather greater distance of course.

Figure 6.2 shows what happens at the speaker's edge to cause the difference. Mic choice can be any dynamic or capacitor that you think sounds good. Bear in mind that it may have to cope with high levels without distortion. Also, if you use a dynamic, remember that it will pick up hum from the amp's transformer. Look round the back to see whether the mains cable goes in on the left or right and position the mic on the opposite side.

The guitar amp is angled so that the sound it produces doesn't fire directly at any other mic in the studio. Remember that the less unwanted 'spill' each mic picks up, the cleaner each track will be on the multitrack tape, which makes life easier for you. Acoustic screens are a great help in reducing spill. They are not very thick, as sound insulators go, but they do reduce the annoyance frequencies significantly. Screens come in a variety of types and it's a simple job to make your own with chipboard, foam, and covering material. Large screens with windows are better at sound insulation, but they tend to make the musicians feel isolated from each other. Half height screens are less obtrusive, and still keep their effect because most of the sound is being produced near to the studio floor.

Many bass guitarists do without an amp these days and direct inject the signal from the bass straight into the console. If you have good EQ on your console, direct injection will work well, perhaps with a little compression too. If your console has only average EQ, and unfortunately even today most consoles are lacking in this department compared to what is possible, then an amp will make the bass sound a lot more butch and beefy. Combining the miked up signal from the amp with a DI feed can give the best of both worlds. With both the guitar and bass amplifiers, it is often useful to employ two mics, one very close and one more distant. The close mic picks up a clean sound with very little spill from other instruments, the more distant mic picks up a fuller, more rounded, tone. Mix them together according to personal taste.

The keyboard instruments are the easiest to deal with because

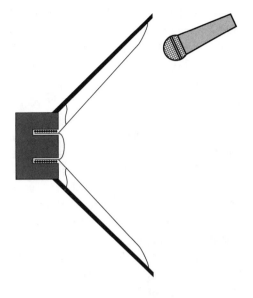

Fig 6.2 The cone of a guitar amp speaker is not as flexibly attached around the edge as a hi fi speaker. This means that as the cone moves in and out, it bends, producing distortion. A mic placed close to the edge will pick up this distortion, which can actually sound quite pleasant

they are usually DI'd into the console. You can use an amplifier if you wish which can help the synthesised sounds blend in with 'real' instruments better, it's up to you.

The one last important member of the band's line up is the vocalist. Although the vocals will be recorded for real later on (involving much time, blood, sweat and tears), it is usually necessary to have a guide vocal on tape right from the start. This not only helps the band while they are laying down the basic track, it helps you judge what the finished result will be like and allows you to think ahead to what problems may occur later on. The vocalist can go anywhere he, or she, feels comfortable as long as there is no spill into any of the instrument mics. If the guide vocals spill over onto other tracks at too high a level, then they may be audible in the final mix. You may get away with it, according to how well the guide is performed, but it's not worth the risk. The singer may decide to change the vocal line later and any guide vocal spill will be ruthlessly exposed.

Once the band are happy with their instruments and amplifiers, and you are happy with the mics (as well as miking the instruments, it's a good idea to set up an extra mic in the centre of the room over which the band will talk to you when they are not playing), you can bring out the headphones and give each band member a pair. A good studio should have at least two circuits for headphone foldback giving the possibility of alternative foldback mixes (usually for the drummer's benefit). Before you disappear into the control room, tell the band – above the noise they are probably making by now – that you'll be a few minutes setting up the headphone balance and suggest that they give the song a run through while they wait.

While the band are busy running through the song and having last minute arguments over minor details, you'll be checking each channel with the solo button and setting the mic gain. Write the name of each instrument onto the console's scribble strip with a wax pencil (Chinagraph) before going on to the next channel. (You will have done this for the drums already while you were working with the drummer alone). With this done, but no faders up as yet, you can turn up the foldback on all the instruments so the band can hear what they are doing through the headphones. Listen to the foldback mix yourself on headphones and set up what you think is a good balance.

When you think all is well, ask the band – over the headphones – and they'll tell you what they think of your efforts. A good foldback balance is one of the keys to getting a good performance. It's a very unnatural thing to play wearing headphones, but it has to be done for the sake of the guide vocal, which is usually essential. The musicians will have to negotiate a compromise between what they all would like, since it's unlikely there will be enough separate foldback circuits for all. It's up to you to watch that the level in the cans doesn't get louder and louder, but as you add level to some instruments, you bring down others. If you don't do this, you'll end up with distortion in the headphones and deaf ears all round.

Routing

How many tracks do you have? Eight, sixteen and twenty-four are all good numbers, but let's stick to eight and sixteen track operation for the moment. On eight track, you need to limit the number of tracks for the basic recording to just six (plus the guide), perhaps like this:

Track 1)	Snare or bass drum
Track 2)	Drums left
Track 3)	Drums right
Track 4)	Bass
Track 5)	Guide vocal
Track 6)	-
Track 7)	Guitar
Track 8)	Keyboards

Whether you isolate the snare or bass drum on Track 1 depends on which you think is the most important to the song. All the other drums and cymbals will have to be mixed into stereo at this stage. With sixteen tracks to play with, the options are more open:

Track 1)	-
Track 2)	Bass drum
Track 3)	Snare drum
Track 4)	Tom 1
Track 5)	Tom 2
Track 6)	Tom 3
Track 7)	Overhead left
Track 8)	Overhead right
Track 9)	Hihat
Track 10)	Bass
Track 11)	Guitar
Track 12)	Keyboard
Track 13)	Guide vocal
Track 14)	-
Track 15)	-
Track 16)	-

This only leaves four tracks for vocals and overdubs so you might want to condense it a little (you'll know which way to go from your earlier discussions with the band):

Track 1)	-
Track 2)	Bass drum
Track 3)	Snare drum
Track 4)	Drums left
Track 5)	Drums right
Track 6)	Bass
Track 7)	Guitar
Track 8)	Keyboard
Track 9)	Guide vocal
Track 10)	-
Track 11)	-
Track 12)	-
Track 13)	-
Track 14)	-
Track 15)	-
Track 16)	-

This has much more room for plenty of extra musical interest, and the result can sound technically just as good as the first layout – but you have to get the drums right now. There's no margin for error here. One nicety that you might notice is that Track 1 hasn't been used yet in either of the 16-track track lists. This is because the edge

Modular digital multitracks

At the highest level of recording studios, analogue 2-inch 24-track and digital DASH machines are common and will remain in use for the foreseeable future. In home and project studios, and elsewhere, 8-track modular digital multitracks (MDMs) have become very popular. The ADAT (originated by Alesis) and DTRS (originated by Tascam) MDMs are reasonably priced and several can easily be synchronised together to form a 16, 24 or 32-track system – even bigger if you wish. The main drawback is that synchronisation takes a little time, although the DTRS system is pretty fast. Everything in this chapter can be applied to any type of multitrack recorder, although with an MDM system you may want to bear in mind that operation slows down once you exceed eight tracks and a second machine is brought into operation. MDMs that use optical disk cartridges are now available and synchronisation, at least in theory, should be instant.

tracks of any multitrack tape are prone to damage or drop out. It's more likely than you think, even with modern machinery. If it does cause a problem, then it had better happen to a minor instrument where it can go unnoticed or be mixed down in level. The instruments being recorded now are all important and need the protection of being on the inner tracks. You could, however, allocate the guide vocal to an edge track if you wanted, because it won't be used in the final mix. This is because the edge tracks of any analogue multitrack tape are prone to damage or drop out. Digital multitracks are unaffected by this.

As you allocate each instrument to a tape track, you need to write it in on a track sheet. This is usually just a sheet of paper or card with as many boxes as tape tracks. I prefer to use something like Figure 6.3. This gives me space to change things, for example if one instrument is replaced by another, or if several are combined onto one track to make room for more work. Make no mistake about trusting this sort of information to memory. It's so easy to erase a track by accident, and musicians can be very unforgiving about this.

When you and the band are ready for a take and have set up levels and a monitor balance, ask the guitarist and bassist to tune to the keyboard (or if they have an electronic tuner, so much the better). In the old days before synths were digitally controlled and stable, I used to record a tuning note before anything else then whenever there was any doubt about tuning, there was always an absolute reference available. A tuning note on tape also comes in handy if you are going to mess about with varispeed – more on this later. Once you are tuned it's time to begin. Get the band to count in audibly onto the tape for the benefit of future overdubs, and then you are into Take 1.

Getting a good solid backing track is very important in this type of

TITLE:				
1				
2				
3				
4				
5				
6				
7				
8				
9				
10				
11				
12				
13				
14				
15				
16				
NOTES:				

Fig 6.3 A track sheet can simplify things considerably

recording. Sequenced MIDI recording tends to progress gradually, track by track, but here you are covering several steps with one giant bound. If the backing track is not perfect, then there is no hope of success. Perfection here means no wrong notes, no drum sticks clashing together, consistent tempo and a good 'feel'. Even if you record over bad takes, you may end up with three or four good ones from which, in consultation with the band, to choose the best. It is in theory possible to edit the multitrack tape so that you can combine the best bits of two or more takes. This depends on the tempo being consistent between the takes, so if you do feel adventurous, check the tempi of the bits you would like to edit together before you cut the tape.

Back in eight track land, once you have a good take it's time for another giant leap. Since you have filled all but two tracks (you will probably have to lose the guide vocal very soon, but it will have served a good purpose while you had it) you will need to mix the six instrumental tracks onto Tracks 5 and 6 (best not to use edge tracks, remember), then do your overdubs onto the tracks you have freed up. Mixing the backing tracks isn't easy because you don't have all the instrumental parts available to make your judgment. But you can listen to the guide vocal right up to the point you commit yourself to the record button. This will help get a good balance. And once you have recorded the backing track onto Tracks 5 and 6 and cleaned up the others there's NO GOING BACK.

Overdubs

From the engineer's point of view, instrumental overdubs can be quite a chore. Especially with keyboards, you can spend a lot of time doing little more than nursing a fader, making sure that the levels on tape are correct. But on the other hand, if the band isn't experienced in recording, they won't know as well as you how precise things must be to ensure a good result. In live work, obviously you don't want to make a mistake, but if you do then you shrug it off in a moment and it's on to the next bit and hope no-one noticed. In a recording, even the smallest mistake will shine through like a beacon telling everyone that there has been a cock up. Perhaps on the first playback it will sound very minor – maybe not all the band will notice it. On the second playback everyone will hear it, on the third and subsequent plays it will grow in magnitude until it's all you can think about. The answer is not to let any blemish get past a first listening.

Spotting mistakes is one thing. On a higher level of skill is the ability to judge whether a take is good enough. When a musician finds his part difficult to get just right, you are faced with having to decide when he has played it to a sufficient standard. Don't forget that it's

Everything you record should be auditioned straightaway to make sure it is good. This means listening in complete silence and in a very concentrated manner. This is very important, it's an art that is only acquired with practice, to be able to listen to a take once only and spot even a small mistake. Casual listening, coupled with chit chat between band members is not nearly good enough.

nearly always the engineer who has the most experience in close listening and in assembling a song from a collection of separately recorded tracks. It's not good practice just to accept a musician's say so, but be as tactful as possible when making comments on the quality of peoples' playing. Make sure that you are satisfied with each overdub before moving on, then you'll get a good end product, the band will be satisfied even on repeated listenings back home and they will come back to you with more business.

When to EQ?

The first answer to this is when you need to! Like tomato sauce, EQ goes better with some things than others. But there is another slant to this question. Do you EQ when you are laying the instruments down onto the multitrack tape, or do you record them flat and EQ during the mix? Both alternatives have their pros and cons. Without exposing my bias, here they are:

EQ during track laying

For: Boosting particular frequencies adds noise to the signal. If the EQ is added before the signal goes onto the tape, then there is less noise to be boosted. Musicians respond to the sounds they hear on the tape when they add their overdubs. If these sounds are optimised with EQ, and perhaps with effects too, they will be responding to sounds which are close to how they will be in the final mix, resulting in a more cohesive overall sound.

Against: What's done can not always be undone. If you cut particular frequencies, trying to put them back later will not be possible without adding a lot of noise.

No EQ during track laying

For: The signal is left in a pure state right up to the mix. Only when you mix do you have all the information available on which to make your judgements.

Against: The recording may sound as though it is not 'coming along' properly making you and the musicians anxious about the quality of the end result.

There is of course a compromise position. During recording, you add the EQ that you are certain that the track will need, not doing anything too drastic. Often this can simply mean rolling off excess bass on instruments which are not bass instruments. This can clean up a recording considerably and may be all the EQ you need much of the time. In a similar way, these comments are also relevant to reverb. You could add some reverb during the process of recording the basic tracks, but it limits your options later. Remember that you can add reverb easily, but it's very difficult to take it away.

Effects

Guitarists tend to carry a bag full of effects pedals with them which can vary in quality from very good to perfectly awful. Whatever you think about the superiority of the effects units in your rack, you have to remember that the musician may just know what is best. If a guitarist suggests that he wants to use an effect (or more likely plugs one in without talking to you about it) have a careful listen to the sound it makes. If you really think you can get the same effect, but at a higher level of quality with your effects rack, then mention it to him and give it a try. It may be however that even though the foot pedal effect is noisy, crackly and just plain cheap, it's giving the guitarist the sound he wants. In this case you just have to clean it up as best you can with EQ and noise gating.

7 | Recording drums

If you like a challenge, then you will probably enjoy recording drums more than any other instrument. It's human nature to respond to a challenge, and when it comes to this supremely complex collection of sound producing apparatus, a few top engineers have responded by achieving results so amazingly good that it would take years of experience even to come close — assuming that you have the good acoustics and first class equipment that are also necessary. Despite this, a little knowledge can go a long way. As long as you don't expect a drum sound that will rip the diaphragm out of your abdomen at the first attempt, a few well tried and tested techniques and ideas will help you to get a good professional sound.

The kit

Of all the instruments, the engineer needs to know most about the drum kit, and will have the most influence over the way it is set and played. Try telling a guitarist or a bassist how they should plug in their instrument and how they should play and they will probably think that you are getting too big for your Doc Martens, unless you already have a good working relationship. But whatever the drummer thinks about your involvement with his kit and the way he is playing it, it is extremely important to the end result.

Unless the drummer is experienced in studio work, most of his effort will have gone towards getting a good live sound. Now is the time to persuade him that you want things done differently. First, let's look at the drums of the kit individually and see what we can do with them...

Bass drum

Americans call this the Kick Drum because once upon a time it was played by simply giving it a good hard thwack with a size ten boot. Evolution has made matters somewhat more sophisticated, and in fact if you are into high tech heavy engineering, take a look at some of the fancy bass drum pedals that are around these days! The bass drum itself is just a large drum placed on its side with a head (the drum skin) at either end. If that's how it comes into the studio — i.e. with two heads — then you will need to do something because, in this case, two

> Three rules of thumb:
>
> You can't get a good recording of...
>
> 1) a bad kit.
>
> 2) a good kit, badly set up.
>
> 3) a good kit, well set up but played badly (or inappropriately for the song).

heads are not better than one. A double headed bass drum is a great instrument for a Salvation Army band, and in fact it does suit many styles of music well. But for music in the modern idiom it is just too 'boomy', or to be more precise, the sound isn't sharp enough and goes on too long. The remedy is to remove the front head and put a blanket inside. This will give the currently fashionable short sharp thud that we are most times aiming for. An alternative to this, which many drummers will have done already, is to cut a hole in the front head. This is a very acceptable solution too. The hole allows access for the damping material – the blanket – and for the microphone.

Round at the working end of the drum are the pedal and beater. It's always worth taking a look at the beater, it may be hard or soft – giving hard or soft sounds, naturally – or may have one hard and one soft surface and is rotatable. If you check this out before recording starts, you will at least know something more about the kit, and maybe have a valuable option if the bass drum sound needs changing for any reason.

Snare drum

Opinions differ on whether the snare or the bass is the most important drum in the kit, but it's for certain that they are both more important than any other. The snare drum always has two heads. The lower head has, tensioned against it, a number of snare wires, which gives the drum its 'snappy' sound. It's worth spending some time working on the tuning of this drum, because the sound is so vital in its contribution to the whole arrangement.

The drummer will have a key for adjusting the tensioners around the rim of the drum. Some recording engineers have their own drum key too – just in case the drummer forgets. Drum tuning is a bit of an art, so you should let the drummer apply the motive force while you comment on the sound he is getting. Usually, the snare is tensioned evenly all round. The choice is between a higher or lower pitch, always aiming at a sound with which the drum itself sounds comfortable (because of the dimensions of the shell), and which hopefully will suit the arrangement of the music.

Just like bass drums, snare drums need to be damped. Many snare drums have internal damping mechanisms, which are good for absolutely nothing. The way to damp a snare drum to get a shorter snappier sound is to gaffer tape a piece of cotton wool to the top head. The sound will be affected by the quantity of damping material and its positioning, so work out with the drummer what sounds best. Sometimes the snare wires need a bit of damping too to prevent them from rattling too loudly in sympathy with the other drums in the kit.

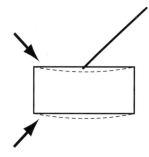

Fig 7.1 Double miking a snare drum (side view)

The snare drum is usually considered to be fairly important, so much so that it is sometimes given two mics. The snare drum actually produces an approximately equal amount of sound from both sides, because of the snare wires on the bottom head. It is often worthwhile to put a mic under the drum to pick up the snares and mix it in with the mic on top. But unless you know a little trick, it will sound pretty awful. Let me explain..

As you can see from Figure 7.1, when the stick hits the top head it moves downwards, away from the top mic. The pressure of the air inside the drum makes the bottom head move down too, towards the bottom mic. If these were mixed together as they are, the output from the two mics would be out of phase, and result in a cancellation of the fundamental frequency of the drum, making it sound weak. Fortunately, there is a simple answer: Hit the phase button on one of the channels on the mixer. so that the outputs of the two mics reinforce one other, giving a strong sound combining the stick hit with the snare rattle.

Toms

Toms fall into two categories: double headed and single headed (sometimes called concert toms), and usually all the toms in any one kit will be of the same type. Unlike the situation with the bass drum, there isn't so much preference from the recording point of view. A good tom is a good tom, the only point being that concert toms give you an extra option when it comes to miking - you can mic them from below.

Usually, the function of the toms is to give the drummer the opportunity to play a thundering roll across all of them at a particularly dramatic point in the music, so you want the sound to be powerful. Once again, the tuning key comes out – either the drummer's or yours. There are two tuning requirements for toms, apart from the essential point that whatever pitch the head is tuned to, it should suit the size of the shell. Listening to all the toms, there should be an equal musical interval between each drum. You don't need an electronic tuner to judge this, nor do you have to tune them to any other instrument of the band, as long as a roll around the toms sounds good. The other point about tom tuning is that if the head is unevenly tensioned, the pitch will fall during the duration of the note, and this is what actually gives the tom its characteristic sound. Hopefully the drummer will know how to do this for best effect, but even if he doesn't, at least you have given him something to think about and experiment with before the next session.

Cymbals

Arrgh! The curse of the recording engineer strikes again! If it wasn't for the cymbals it would be so much easier to get a good drum sound, but those drummers got in first on the act, before recording was invented, so we have to cope with them as best we can. A typical drum kit will have a minimum of four cymbals: crash, ride, and a pair of hihats. Crash and ride cymbals perform different functions for the drummer (one accentuates, the other supports the sound) but they are not usually treated any differently when it comes to recording.

As I said earlier, you are onto a loser if the drum kit isn't up to much. With cymbals, the problem is even greater. It seems that less than perfect drums can be tweaked up with appropriate mic positioning and EQ into something decent, if not wonderful. But bad cymbals always sound like dustbin lids. The hihat is especially important since it is the third most important component of the kit after the bass and snare drums. My own solution to drummers with poor cymbals was to buy my own pair of hihat cymbals (Paiste 2002 Sound Edge 14") which I can't play to save my life, although I keep them on a stand to amuse visitors to my flat.

Mic technique

In my trip round the kit I have missed out one thing – that the drums will rattle like crazy until you liberally apply gaffer tape to the fixtures and fittings. But after that, you are ready to put up some microphones. But where, and how many? There are, to my mind, two ways to mic up drums. One is to use as few mics as possible, the other is to use as many as you can think of positions for. In between stages can only result in compromises on some of the instruments of the kit. Let me explain...

Obviously the smallest number of mics you can use on any instrument is two, if you want stereo. Two isn't quite enough for drums, and Figure 7.2 a and b show why. The best place for two of the mics has to be above the kit, but this leaves the bass drum rather far away and isolated so you need one more. The two overhead mics are placed behind the kit so they don't pick up too much cymbal (although they'll still get plenty). Cymbals are directional and radiate most from their flat surfaces, so if the mics are as nearly as possible in line with the edges, they won't pick

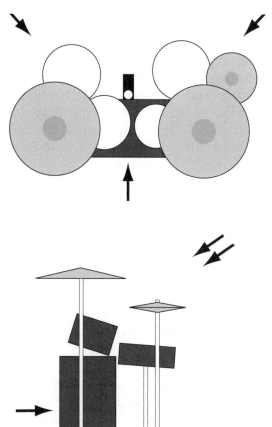

Fig 7.2a Three mics on the drum kit (viewed from above)

Fig 7.2b Same three mics viewed from the side

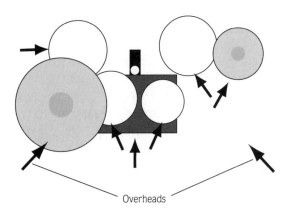

Fig 7.3 Multiple microphone setup
(cymbal removed to show snare mic)

Overheads

up so much. Rest assured that with this arrangement, there is never any shortage of cymbal. When positioning the mics, don't go below the drummers shoulder level or he will screen off part of the kit.

The positioning of the bass drum mic gives the engineer a few options: the closer it is to the beater, the harder the sound will be. The further away it is, the more of the sound of the shell of the drum it will pick up. Experiment!

Perhaps you are thinking now, 'If three mics are good, won't four be better?'. The answer is yes, but problems arise. The obvious place for a fourth mic would be on the snare. But now the toms will be at a disadvantage, so you put mics on the toms, and pretty soon you have got a mic on every drum on the kit. In fact it really is the only other way to go – one mic per drum plus one on the hihat and a pair of overheads, as in Figure 7.3. I don't need to say that it is difficult to balance all these mics, and it is impossible to learn how to do it apart from by experience, but I can offer some guidelines:

Method 1)
Get a sound on the overheads and bass drum. Then bring up each mic in turn until it fits in with the general sound. Use headphones to pan each mic precisely to the same position as it appears to be in the stereo image of the overheads.

Method 2)
Start with the bass drum only, then bring in the snare, then the other mics in turn. When the individual mics are balanced, bring up the overheads to fill in the cymbals.

With these two methods, you will tend to get different results. The first will give a fairly natural sound, but stronger than the three mic set up. The second will be more powerful, but is harder to deal with and requires careful mic positioning. There is a third method:

Method 3):
Bring up the faders to random levels and work it out from there! This may seem haphazard, but believe it or not, it is a valuable mixing technique, and works when you are mixing down the complete track to stereo too. I wouldn't use it as a first option though.

So far, everything is going smoothly. But that's because you are reading a book and not doing it for real! As you know, there can be a world of difference between theory and practice. What will happen in real life is that a selection of problems will crop up at each stage. Here are a few:

The drums don't sound very crisp.
For crispness you need to use a capacitor microphone. The Neumann U87 for instance is very good, as are some other expensive models.

The toms sound weak, even when I push the faders right up.
For powerful toms, dynamic mics are best. Capacitor mics can give a very accurate sound, but do you want an accurate representation of what it's like to have your ear an inch from a drum head? Dynamic mics round off the fastest transients, which you can hardly hear anyway, and allow the real power to come through.

The more mics I put up on the faders, the more it seems to muddy the sound.
This is because every mic you put out picks up every drum in the kit. It is bound to create a bit of a muddle. The best thing to do is to follow the 10:1 rule which states that the second closest mic to any drum must be at least 10 times as far away as the closest.

When I bring up the high tom mic, the snare sound goes all funny.
Aha! Sounds like the mics are picking up an out of phase signal on the snare. This happens by chance because of the relationship between the distances from the snare to the snare mic and from the snare to the tom mic, and the fundamental frequency produced by the snare drum. Press the phase button on the mixer for one of the mics and it should cure the problem (but be aware that the same problem may have now moved elsewhere).

Doing it better

Recording drums and getting them to sound like a real kit being played by a real drummer isn't easy. As I have indicated, it takes a lot of experience to get the feel of whether a certain mic can be placed an inch up or down, whether you should ask the drummer to tune a drum differently, or even play it differently etc. There are, however, tricks of the trade to help you get better results, providing that they don't work to the detriment of the music, and also providing that the drummer is willing and able. If you want to get a better drum sound, by which I mean clearer and more powerful, and with better dynamics, then the number one thing to do is get rid of the dustbin lids – sorry, I mean cymbals. If we can do that, we get rid of a sound that is leaking into all our drum mics, and we will also be able to lower the overheads and pick up the individual drums more clearly. Even a simple three mic arrangement can give a really good clear sound if there are no cymbals in the way. Obviously, if the arrangement calls for a lot of subtle interplay between drums and cymbals, then you can't do it like this. But very often it is possible to do the cymbal crashes as overdubs. You might even find that the drummer likes working this way.

One step further along the same path is to get rid of the hihat too, and overdub that. Most drummers have their hihat very close to the snare, and inevitably a lot of its sound will leak into the snare mic – in fact you may not need to use a hihat mic at all. It cleans up the sound even more to do away with the hihat, but the problem is that it may be impossible for the drummer to play the hihat as an overdub and get the rhythm precise enough. Even if it might be possible, the drummer may not be cooperative because he sees it as 'cheating' and a devaluation of his role. Of course, it's up to you to get the best sound by using appropriate techniques and being as persuasive as you can.

Once the drums, mics and mixing console are set up to your satisfaction, it's all systems go, but remember that the drum kit is the foundation of the arrangement. Listen closely to the sounds the kit is making and to the accuracy of the drummer's rhythm. Don't hesitate to speak up if you think that something can be improved, or if the rhythm sags even momentarily. And while you are listening to the throbbing sound of the drums going down onto tape, just remember that you won't have this much fun again in the studio – until you do the vocals!

Recording vocals

The human voice can be the most difficult instrument to record, bar none. But despite that, the human voice can actually be reasonably easy and straightforward to deal with in the studio – providing that you have a brilliant singer who is well experienced in recording, and all the necessary tools such as a good mic, good acoustics and good studio equipment. But good singers – good in the studio that is – are very hard to come by, harder even than good drummers. There are plenty of average vocalists about, and plenty of pretty good ones, but the sort that you can just place in front of a microphone and record in a couple of takes are worth their weight in platinum – and that's practically what it takes to pay them for session work.

So what exactly do I mean by 'good vocalist'? The first requirement is to be able to learn the tune quickly, and learn it well enough to put expression into the words and music. The second requirement is to be able to sing in tune all the time, even when wearing headphones. This is probably the factor that will cause more headaches than any other. Put it this way, if your vocalist sings in tune, then you won't have to spend hour upon hour doing drop-ins, retakes, 'fixes' and whatever else it needs to get the performance right, bearing in mind that you are struggling against time as the performer's voice gradually deteriorates. Once again, more on this later.

Another requirement for any vocalist is the valuable personal asset of being able to do exactly what is asked. Obviously this doesn't apply so much to the likes of Michael Jackson and Madonna who can hire and fire more recording engineers in a week than you or I can spit cherry stones. 'The ability to take direction' is a more appropriate way to say it. There are many musicians who are only too willing to do their best for you and play or sing in exactly the way you want, but willingness alone doesn't get the job done. The ability to take direction means that what you ask for, you get, performance-wise, and is not necessarily related to the amount of backchat you are likely to get.

I could go on rhapsodising about the merits of using a really good vocalist, but if some are that good, why is modern music populated with singers who can't tell the difference between an A sharp and a Z blunt? The history of popular music through the ages from Bob Dylan to Bob Geldof is littered with singers who, by any objective criterion,

Really good vocalists and musicians will not only do exactly what you want them to, they will also add suggestions of their own and give you not just 100% of what you asked, but 150% or more.

just can't sing. The answer to this conundrum is that singing is more than simply articulating a tune and a rhythm, it's more about putting across an idea or a feeling. And some people who can't do the former very well are very good at the latter, and ideas and feelings are more important than the mere nuts and bolts of the music.

What all this boils down to in practical terms for the recording engineer, is that you are more likely than not to be dealing with singers who are not at the technical level of being able to turn in a top-notch performance every time. They may be able to put the idea across, but need a lot of help from the engineer to do it in a musically acceptable way. If you look at it like this, it's not so much that recording the vocals is a troublesome task which takes a lot of time, sweat and tears – it's a part of the creative process in which the engineer can play a very full and active role. It's an exciting moment when a vocal comes together on tape and it has all the elements of an artistically worthwhile and technically perfect musical performance. The next question is, 'How is it done?'

Preparation

The situation I am going to look at is where the engineer/producer has written or otherwise come by a song and has asked a vocalist to come in and record it for him. Recording a singer in a band involves all the same processes, but the engineer would probably not have quite as much say in the proceedings. As in many things, preparation is essential, and the first stage in preparation is for the singer to learn the song. As you would expect, some people are faster learners than others. I have known singers who can pick up a song after just a couple of run throughs, and I have known others who just don't seem to have the ability to learn new songs!

The best way to do it is to make a rough version of the song and give the vocalist a cassette a few days before the session. Obviously, it has to have a vocal on it, but even if it isn't totally in tune, it must put the song over the way you want to hear it, with the correct feeling. It's best to ask the singer what he or she thinks of the key, too high or too low. Even if you have to do some rearrangement and rerecording of the backing track, it's well worth while to have the song pitched correctly for the singer you are using. The right pitch is obviously when the song falls within the singer's range without too much straining for high and low notes. If you know the singer well, then it may be possible to go for a high key which you know could never be performed live, but can be pieced together in the recording. If it's a first time though, play safe – there's enough to go wrong without asking the singer to tighten his jockstrap a couple of notches.

Learning the song is a matter of learning the tune and learning the rhythm of the words. The way the words fit a song is important, especially as they change from verse to verse. There is a world of difference between lyrics that fit and lyrics that don't. Often, lyrics can be made to fit perfectly by singing them in a certain way. If you know how it should be done, make sure that it's done that way on the rough demo so that the singer doesn't have to relearn it in the studio.

The other aspect to preparation concerns work in the studio. For instance, what time of day do you intend to record the vocal? In the morning, afternoon or evening? Funnily enough, most singers don't like working very much in the morning. I know that this applies to most of us, but it is to do with physical reasons, not that they can't get out of bed. Most people's voices tend to rise in pitch during the day. It's an interesting experiment to try out on yourself – match the lowest note you can sing to your keyboard early in the morning, and do the same just before bedtime. There may be a difference of as many as seven or eight semitones.

Whatever time of day the session takes place, it's good to have some 'hospitality' ready for your singer's arrival. This may range from a can of beer to a bottle of gin (not too large!), or it may just mean a ready supply of mineral water, whatever keeps the throat well lubricated. Some singers insist on lubricating their throats with cigarette smoke and, whatever your feelings on the subject, you would be unwise to risk compromising the performance by banning smoking in your studio (which is actually a good idea otherwise because the smoke, when it settles, contaminates and reduces the life expectancy of your equipment). Conversely, if you smoke and the singer doesn't – well I hope that giving up temporarily won't make you too irritable.

Rehearsal

Before starting any serious work, it's time for a chat with the singer. You may want to chat about the song, about the world situation, interest rates, or about any other subject that takes your fancy. The point of this is to make you both feel more relaxed and able to talk easily, which will be important later. Even if you know each other well, it's rarely possible to dive straight into work and achieve any useful results.

Hopefully, the studio will be set up already, with a selection of microphones on stands ready to be tried out, to see which best matches the singer's voice. The choice of microphones for vocals is a strange thing. Whereas most engineers will have favourite mics for the various different instruments, it is impossible to have just one favourite mic for vocals and use it all the time. There is always an interaction between voice and mic, which is especially true when the two are used very close together. Some voices will sound fine on Mic A and terrible on Mic B, other voices vice-versa. Sometimes the same person will sound good on one mic one day, and good on another mic the next day. Until someone invents a grand unified theory of vocal miking there is but one solution - try them all out.

When it comes to vocal miking, there are two Grade 1 champs, and a number of lesser contenders. Probably the most used mic for vocals is the Neumann U87. It's not exactly a new design, but it does the business, as does the AKG C414. The number three vocal mic, which for some unaccountable reason hasn't been in production for a quite a few years, is the Neumann U47 - the VALVE U47 that is. Many engineers swear by the valve '47, and the current model of U47 with FETs (Field Effect Transistors) instead of valves is a pretty powerful performer too.

What studio vocal mics tend to have in common is that they are mostly large diaphragm capacitor mics, so it's a pretty good bet to try any you can lay your hands on such as the Beyer MC740 or AKG 'The Tube'. Even if it means a hire bill, it's worth it. Small diaphragm capacitor mics such as the Neumann KM84 or AKG C451, I find, don't have it when it comes to the human voice. In theory, a small diaphragm should be more accurate, but it's the ultimate result according to the ear that's important, not the spec sheet.

Dynamic mics can also be useful for vocals. The Shure SM57 and 58 are classics, as is the Electrovoice RE20 (the world's ugliest mic), and can have the right sound for certain types of music, particularly rock music but they can never be as 'crisp' as a capacitor. Whatever mics you have available, it is well worth having two or three set up so you can have a quick listen at each and make a choice. It's not usually wise to appear to be 'messing about' with either the mics or the positioning. Musicians tend to see this as unprofessional, even though it's a vital part of the engineer's art, and this may compromise the performance.

The mic position can have a great effect on the sound of the voice. Distances from zero to about a metre are useful – more if you are recording an opera singer in a large room. The further away, normally, the more natural the sound; the closer to the mic, the more present and intimate the singer appears – it can be like whispering in your ear. Of course, the closer the singer gets, the more chance there is of the mic 'popping'. This happens on consonants such as 'p' and 'b' where a jet of fast moving air bursts from the lips and blasts the diaphragm. Popping is nearly always fatal to the recording. Even with a heavy bass roll-off it can usually still be heard when the song is mixed, so it's definitely something to avoid.

The Shure SM 58 – one of the classic rock 'n' roll microphones

There are two ways to deal with popping. The first is for the singer to sing across rather than directly at the microphone and to ease off on the offending consonants. The other is to use a pop shield. Most mics have accessory wind shields which are either supplied with the mic or are available as an extra and simply fit onto the business end of the mic. These are great for keeping spit out of the mic and for working outdoors, but they don't do much for popping, unfortunately.

The best tool for dealing with popping comes absolutely free and consists of two components: a wire coat hanger (free with your dry cleaning) and a length of nylon stocking (free when you ask nicely). I'll leave the mechanical arrangements up to you, but basically the requirement is for a lightly stretched membrane eight to ten inches across positioned in front of the mic. Stocking material is full of holes and will allow sound to pass through unimpeded, except at very low frequencies – the popping frequencies – which are absorbed by the membrane and will not blast the mic, or at least will blast it a lot less.

Choosing the mic, setting it and adjusting the pop shield can all be done while the singer is running through the track. 'Running through' doesn't mean the same as 'rehearsing', it's just a way of getting used to the song, the setting and a time to get things, including headphone foldback, basically right. The rehearsal period itself is where serious work starts, the vocalist starts to sing out and the engineer sets levels and fine tunes the foldback mix.

It is worth taking a closer look at foldback and the best way of doing it. Obviously, the singer has to hear the backing track, and him or herself, in the headphones. The headphone volume has to be at the right level, and also the mix of the instruments. The foldback mix may not have all the instruments in it, just enough to give the rhythm and tuning. Although most consoles are geared up to having a mono foldback mix, it really is best to have it in stereo, which simply means using two aux sends. The level of the voice in the foldback mix is important. Singers react to what they hear, and if the amount of voice is too much, it's possible that he or she will ease off slightly. The singer may ask for more level, but while accommodating their requests, think also about what they really need.

When the engineer has such a range of effects as are available in the modern studio, it is tempting to use a few of them while recording the vocal. I'm not going to say don't do it, but simply point out the options. If you have rackfuls of effects units, then there isn't really much point in recording any effect, compression, reverb etc, with the voice – do it on the monitor while recording, and for real in the mix. A flat dry recording of the voice allows much more opportunity later. If you don't have so many effects, then it may be useful to do

The AKG C414 - does the business as a vocal mic

some basic work on the voice while recording.

Nearly always, vocals need a little EQ and compression so it is OK to EQ and compress onto tape, but not too much! Gating onto tape is more dodgy. You will want to gate the vocal track because it always picks up a lot of clutter, breaths, headphone spill and the like, but gating as you record risks losing odd syllables which you may come to regret. Adding effects like reverb or echo depends on the nature of the recording too much for me to comment, but as a rule it's better to leave it for later. Whatever you do about reverb, send some of it to the foldback mix. Reverb on the vocal is an enormous help to the singer. Even the best vocalists can't keep in tune unless they can hear themselves in the headphones clearly, and having a bit of reverb really makes a difference.

When it gets to rehearsal proper, after thinking about all of these points, it's time to check that all is going well, that the singer is singing in tune and in the correct rhythm. If the tuning is suspect, the first thing to suggest is that the singer moves one side of the head-phones slightly away from the ear, so some of the natural sound of the voice gets through.

It is difficult to hear tuning on headphones, so this improves mat-ters. With some singers, it is a problem for them to come in on the right note. There is only one answer to this, if you discount singing lessons (which can actually do more for a vocal performance than any amount of studio trickery), which is to record tuning notes on the tape at strategic points. This may seem like a chore, but time spent doing this can be a valuable investment in some cases.

In the case of the rhythm of the lyrics, if all does not seem to be going smoothly, then a good trick is to mark on the lyric sheet the points at which the singer should breathe. I do it like this:

/ This is the first line / of the song / it's all rather slow/ and long / so the singer needs / a lot of / breath / To manage the / sustained / notes

Apologies for the quality of the lyric, but I can assure you that the method works and has an added advantage in that the gaps in the vocal line will be in exactly the same place in each take, which is good for drop-ins.

Recording

There are two basic techniques for recording any overdub, including vocals. One, which I shall call 'assembly' uses only one track. The other, 'compilation' needs several. As you can see, it's no good record-ing 23 tracks leaving only one free for the vocal and then expecting to use the compilation technique. Let's look at the more economical assembly technique first.

If you have a brilliant vocalist, then you will be able to record all the way through the song and then just drop in a few corrections. But if the vocalist is only average, remembering that even for a good singer it's much harder to record than to perform live, then it can be very depressing when you have several goes at the song, all of which seem virtually useless. The answer is to break the song down into smaller parts. Get a bit of it right, then carry on. If I use this technique to record — I once used it on a song with an extremely difficult vocal line which the singer hadn't an earthly chance of learning in its entirety in the time available — I would probably aim at getting the first two lines right. This may take five takes, ten takes or forty takes (no exaggeration) until it sounds good. I actually swap between two tracks of the tape, so that when I have a good version, I can always get the singer to try for a better one without losing the first. With a good first two lines, confidence builds and the rest of the song tends to go more smoothly.

I won't deny that it's a slog to work in this way, or that it will produce the most perfect, flowing, vocal line, but I do promise that with enough patience it is nearly always possible to get a usable vocal, even with a less than perfect singer.

Compilation needs a reasonably good singer to start with. The aim is to go for complete takes of the whole song, possibly about six of them. From these six takes it should be possible to compile one perfect version by bouncing down into another track. Sounds easy? Well first of all , the singer has to have enough technique to be able to sing all the takes with the same energy and with the same tone of voice, otherwise they won't match when they are compiled. Secondly, it can be a big job just choosing which parts of which take you are going to use. Well no-one said that it was going to be easy to record vocals so here goes...

What you need for the selection procedure is either six copies of the lyrics (or as many as you did takes), or six different coloured pens or pencils. Then as the song plays through, starting with the first take, you mark down the quality rating of lines as A, B, C or X. Guess what 'X' means. It does take a bit of practice to get used to doing this, to assess a line very quickly, mark it, and then get on to the next without stopping the tape.

If both you and the vocalist take part in this exercise, you should be able to come up with a happy compromise eventually. After doing this, it's time for the play offs, where you compare line by line, judging one (hopefully) high quality line against another. After an eternity, you'll have a list which you can put together into a single perfect track, maybe with just a couple of drop ins to fix it completely.

With either recording procedure there will be problems. Here are a few typical examples:

You need to comment on the singer's performance
Develop a selection of platitudes for all occasions such as...

'That was great but...'
'I think you should have another go at that.'
'I know you can do it better.'
'Let's try that again.'
'One more time.'
'That was the best yet, let's try for one better.'

The sound is inconsistent between takes
The singer is probably moving around. Explain the problem carefully and you'll get a better result. If the singer is coming in and out of the control room, it can be worthwhile to mark the floor so he or she always goes back to the same spot.

The vocalist consistently sings a phrase flat
If a phrase keeps on coming out flat and you know it and the singer knows it, suggest that he or she tries to sing sharp, not in tune but sharp. It won't come out right first time, but once the boundaries of the correct pitch have been explored thoroughly from both sides, the next take might be spot on.

"The 'feel' of the vocal isn't right
This is a tough one. One trick that sometimes works is to suggest that the vocalist tries to imagine a mood appropriate to the song – romantic, energetic, aggressive etc – rather than simply what it feels like to be put on the spot in front of a cold unfriendly microphone.

Rare talent

There are two qualities that the recording engineer/producer should cultivate which are of prime importance in recording vocals.

The first is to be able to draw a good performance from the vocalist, to watch the performance develop during the run throughs and early takes, and capture it before the edge goes and the voice begins to fade.

The other is to be able to listen to a take and know whether it is perfect, nearly perfect, acceptable or not good enough, and to be able to tell the singer to do it again without damaging their enthusiasm or confidence.

More than any other factor, the vocal performance can make or break a recording. The engineer or producer who can encourage the absolute best out of a singer has a rare talent. It's more than just operating the equipment and following the correct procedures, it involves a musically intimate person-to-person contact that, despite its difficulties, can make recording very satisfying indeed.

9 MIDI and multitrack

MIDI systems will never replace multitrack recording. Well that's a bold statement to open with and one which is guaranteed to raise the hackles of committed MIDI-philes worldwide. But at least at the present state of the art, any MIDI system, no matter how sophisticated, can have its capabilities increased a thousand fold by the addition of even a modest eight track tape recorder. Let me expand on this:

Suppose you have a sampler or multitimbral synth with eight voices, together with a sequencer to drive it. This means that you have the possibility of having eight different sounds on the go at any one time. Add an eight track recorder, which becomes limited to seven tracks due to the necessity for a sync track, then if you wish you can have all eight voices simultaneously sounding on all seven available tape tracks. $8 + 8 + 8 + 8 + 8 + 8 + 8 = 56$ voices.

See what I mean? And if you could sync up the sequencer to the tape with an extra eight voices for the final mixdown, then you would have a grand total of 64 possible different sounds playing at the same time – all originally from the one instrument. With a bigger MIDI system the possibilities are even more vast (far too big for my calculator to cope with).

Of course multitrack recording will not always mean tape. Soon it will mean magnetic hard disk recording (see Chapter 16), at a later date it will mean optical disk recording, and possibly complete integration into a sampling and synthesis system under MIDI control, but multitrack audio recording is a powerful technique now and, however it is achieved, always will be.

Supposing that the end product of our endeavours is going to be music, which is usually thought of as a creative and artistic thing to do, then what we need of our recording system is that it should be as versatile as possible, allowing creativity free rein with very few restrictions.

The combination of MIDI and multitrack can do this. As we shall see, a MIDI system in itself is good for musical experimentation and development. Adding multitrack not only enlarges the artist's palette where colours are mixed and worked together, but also provides the canvas upon which a sound picture may be built up.

Multitrack can't, but MIDI can

As I have already outlined, A MIDI system is inherently limited by the fact that whatever it is being asked to do, it must do everything at the same time. If you are using Program 1 on your effects unit for the synth pad, then you can't simultaneously use Program 99 for the snare drum (not until they develop 'multitimbral' effects units that is). With pure multitrack recording, then it is no problem at all to use one effect when you record onto Track 1, and quite another effect from the same effects unit on Track 2. But multitrack, by itself, has severe limitations:

Since multitrack tape is a linear medium, i.e. it starts at one end and plays through to the other, it allows very little scope for experimentation with the structure and the changes of tempo in a piece of music. These things have to be worked out thoroughly in advance because once the basic tracks are recorded then it's a long way to go back and start again if things are not quite right.

In some ways, this is not a bad thing because it encourages the use of the most powerful system for music editing there is – the human brain. If you can hear the music in your head, and perhaps strum a guitar or plonk away on a keyboard, then the structure of a piece can be worked out to the minutest detail before a note is recorded.

But while this way of working is good for musical geniuses, and for ordinary musicians who don't mind taking the risk of getting trapped into following familiar patterns of thought, the alternative method of improvising then making that improvisation better by polishing, restructuring and making additions, is a powerful way of coming up with new ideas, developing them in new directions, and generally making the best of one's musical abilities.

MIDI systems, incorporating a sequencer, are ideal as an aid to musical creativity because they allow you to start from the germ of an idea and build it up gradually into a finished piece of music, while all the time being available to play back the piece in its current state. It's as though Beethoven had a team of copyists and an orchestra of musicians at the ready while he was writing his symphonies – well almost.

You can begin with something as simple as a two bar drum loop, expand that into an eight bar section, add a bass line and chords, copy that into a new section and alter the parts slightly, create a chorus in the same way, shuffle the sections around, add bits, take way what you don't like – the sequenced MIDI system is as representative of freedom in musical thought as a chunk of concrete hacked off the Berlin Wall is of political freedom.

Synchronisation

MIDI sequencers and multitrack tape recorders of course need to be synchronised together if the music isn't going to be turned into the aural equivalent of scrambled eggs. It almost seems like the dim and distant past when this was thought of as a real problem, but it really is only within the last few years that MIDI sync has got itself properly sorted out. There are basically two options, two sensible options that is.

SMPTE/EBU Timecode

Timecode was originally invented, under the guidance of the Society of Motion Picture and Television Engineers and later the European Broadcasting Union, to assist in video editing but it has also proved to be very useful in audio. Basically, one track of the tape is 'striped' with timecode - which to the recorder appears to be just another audio signal - and the sequencer can be synchronised to that. Hardware sequencers such as the Akai MPC3000 have timecode synchronisation built in. With software sequencers you can use a timecode to MIDI convertor which will allow you to enter the start time and tempo of the song, and any tempo changes. The problem with this is that this information is contained within the timecode to MIDI convertor and is not stored on disk as part of the sequence. It works but it's a bit fiddly.

MIDI Timecode (MTC)

This is a way of converting SMPTE/EBU timecode into a signal that can travel along a MIDI cable. The advantage is that all the start time and tempo information can now be stored as part of the sequence, which is much more convenient. With a computer-based sequencer, you will need to use a MIDI interface that can translate timecode to MTC, and many can these days. Some sequencers also offer MIDI Machine Control (MMC) where the multitrack recorder can be controlled from the sequencer. This isn't always done in a way that is useful so I'll do nothing more than mention it as a possibility.

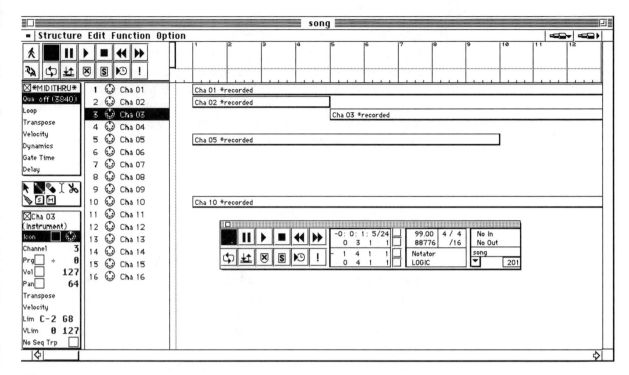

First steps

The first step in creating a piece of music by the MIDI/multitrack method is to get hold of some equipment. But what equipment and how much of it? On the MIDI side, what you need is enough sound producing machinery to get a composition started purely by sequencing, with a wide enough range of sounds to be able to finish it off in the multitrack domain. Rather than dive in and think about the exotic equipment we might like to have, let's think about the music first.

What does the music need? I might say that the minimum would be a drum part, bass line, chords and melody. That implies at least three MIDI synths and a sampler (or fewer if you have a multitimbral synth which has some drum sounds and is easy to use). But you can do a lot with less than this.

With a good sampler, such as the Akai S2000, and a modest synth it's quite possible to sketch out a composition with just drum sounds and a single synth sound on two MIDI channels. Working with the equipment like this in a very simple way gives the brain a chance to work out the music and plan how it will develop, then at a later stage this initial sketch will be gradually coloured in and recorded line by line onto multitrack.

When the outline of the composition is complete, with a finished

Fig 9.1 A computer based sequencer gives a very flexible basis for a MIDI system. This is a screen shot from E-Magic's Notator Logic running on an Apple Mac (photo courtesy *Sound Technology*)

structure and all tempi decided, it's time to get on with some real work – you've had your fun for the moment. Assuming you are starting from square one with your system, then it's time to take out that reel of tape that came free when you bought the multitrack. Since the tape is completely blank, you'll need to stripe it with some timecode (I wonder whether the manufacturers will ever offer us prestriped tape?). Striping simply means recording thirty or so minutes worth of timecode all the way along the tape on the highest numbered track – 8, 16 or 24.

Proceed as follows:

1) Connect a cable from the timecode output of your sequencer to the appropriate input of the multitrack.

2) Select the type of timecode that you wish to use – 25 frames per second is the EBU (European Broadcasting Union) standard, so we might as well be good Europeans and use it, although unless you take the tape to another studio it doesn't really matter which type you use. The generator can be set to start from any time below 23:26:40:00 but for our purposes 00:00:00:00 is quite good enough.

3) With the tape set to Record Ready and any dbx noise reduction set to Off on the timecode track (Dolby C is OK with timecode), start the timecode generator and check the level. It should read around 7dB to 5dB below the zero mark. If it isn't, then you'll have to take steps to adjust it.

If you put the timecode through your mixing console to do this, make sure that there is no EQ and that you disconnect anything concerned with timecode from the mixer before you start on any music. Timecode has a habit of leaking into channels where it isn't wanted, so it's best not to put it into the mixer unless you really have to.

4) With the correct level set, set the tape into Record and start the timecode generator. You now have just over half an hour to enjoy a cup of studio coffee and a leftover sandwich from last night's session.

Once the tape is striped, the next thing to do is to hook up the output of Track 8, 16 or 24 directly to the timecode input of the sequencer, keeping well away from the mixing console, notice. On the sequencer, you'll have to set a Start Time. 00:00:30:00 is about right, a few metres away from the start of the tape.

Now, with your sequencer set to SMPTE/EBU timecode sync, whichever part of the reel you play, the sequencer will read the timecode and convert that to a bar and beat number according to the tempo you have set. If you play the tape from just before the start point, then as 00:00:30:00 is passed, the sequence will start. Magic!

But before we record any sounds onto tape, we may have to add two empty bars at the beginning of the sequence. This is because some sequencers will take a little time to get going. This would throw the rhythm if it happened in the first bar of the music. The second empty bar is so that you get a good four beat metronome count in each time you start, the first bar could be a bit off.

Dump to multitrack

Assuming that the drum sounds you used in the sequence are the ones that you want to use on tape, these will be the first items to be recorded. But in all probability they will all be on the same track of the sequencer, because they were all recorded using the same MIDI channel, so they will have to be separated out. Clever sequencers will do this automatically, but if you have do do it by hand then take care – it's very easy to lose something.

Once you have each drum on a separate sequencer track, preferably with a name, then it's a simple matter to solo each track and record that onto the multitrack, one track at a time. I always have bass drum on Track 2, snare on Track 3, hihat on Track 4, toms on Track 5 etc. (I leave Track 1 blank until I have something of lesser importance to place on it. The edge tracks are always more prone to damage or drop outs).

If your sampler or drum machine has separate outputs which are convenient to use then you can allocate each drum to its own output and record them onto multitrack in one pass. Doing it this way can save a lot of time, but I prefer the one drum at a time approach because I like to add a bit of ambience onto each drum. Not a lot, but just enough to make me think that I recorded a real drum in a real room with a real mic. I may, or may not, add more reverb in the mix.

After the drums, I put down my guide keyboard track onto tape, throw the lever switch in my brain into multitrack mode and get on with some more creativity.

For subsequent tracks, instead of working purely with the sequencer, I have to work with the tape, which means using the tape transport controls to find my way around the music, which is never as convenient as doing it from the sequencer using bar numbers. As we shall see shortly, things won't always be this way. But for the moment, I have to locate the tape to a point just before the head of the track, then when I start it, the sequencer will start too at the correct timecode value and I can record a bass line with a new synth or sampler voice onto a fresh sequencer track.

When the bass line is finished, I dump it onto tape and start with the next layer. So throughout the course of recording, a new track is recorded into the sequencer – which is always syncing to tape – then transferred onto a clear track on the multitrack. Eventually the tape fills up and we have to proceed to phase three of the MIDI/multitrack process.

When the tape has no free tracks left, it is still possible to record extra lines into the sequencer, as many as you have MIDI instruments and free channels on your mixer. These will be played 'live' by the sequencer during mix down to stereo. If I'm using a piano sound on my sampler then I generally like to play this live from the sequencer into the mix because even with a well looked after tape recorder the real thing – well, the real sample – always sounds just a touch cleaner. Other candidates for live playback include anything very trebly which may lose some of its sparkle on tape or sounds which need heavy EQ which may boost tape noise to an unacceptable level.

The real problem with working like this is that it is so much more difficult to find your way around with the tape recorder leading and the sequencer following than it is using the sequencer by itself. This makes it a bit of a nuisance to work out a new part while listening to what you have already on the tape.

One way round this is to use a spare synth set to a fairly neutral sound to play all the tracks you have recorded into the sequencer so far, or whatever tracks you think necessary, by switching them all to the same MIDI channel on the sequencer and setting the synth to that channel. If you can spare a drum machine as well, then this is pretty good for overdubbing to without the hassle of shuttling tape back and forth.

One day the real answer will be to use MIDI Machine Control (MMC) so that you never need to touch the multitrack other than to put the tape in. When all sequencers understand MMC properly, and the way engineers need to use it, we will be able to consider ourselves very fortunate.

An alternative to working on a sketch version of the music to map out the general structure is possible when your MIDI system has reached a level of sophistication where it can produce almost the finished article all by itself, and multitrack is used to add the finishing touches. In this case, a good way of working is to arrange and mix the track, purely in the MIDI domain, into stereo and record it onto two tracks of the multitrack. Extra layers of interest can be added onto the other tracks and then finally mixed onto stereo tape or DAT. There are at least two advantages in working in this way: firstly, it is very easy to keep your eye – or rather your ear – on how the track is going to sound when it's finished, without taking the music apart and putting it on tape strand by strand in the conventional multitrack way. The other advantage is that it's cheap! An eight track recorder is quite sufficient, which can cost several thousand pounds less than the 24-track recorder that would be the minimum necessary for high level work using the one track per instrument method.

Fun?

Yes it is, to combine the flexibility of MIDI with the raw power of multitrack tape. When you consider that a machine like the Alesis ADAT is available at a price not that much higher than one synthesiser of professional standard, and it expands the capabilities of a MIDI system enormously and lets you record guitars and vocals, getting a multitrack is a step that just has to be taken sooner or later.

Looking upmarket to sixteen or twenty four tracks expands the horizons still further, and if you already have a good sampler and a couple of synths then it may be time to start asking whether progressing further in that direction is going to invoke the law of diminishing returns. With a MIDI/multitrack system, you will not only get the best from your existing equipment, you will also get the best from yourself and you'll find that, more than any system which relies solely on the 5-pin DIN, the possibilities are indeed limitless.

Sync problems

The 'P' word comes back to haunt us again. But if you take suitable steps, then problems shouldn't cause too much trouble. The very worst thing that can happen is that for some horrendous reason you lose the sequence. There are a million ways this can happen and it stands to reason, and Murphy's law, that one of them will get you in the end.

Try this with your computer, sampler or sequencer or anything that stores onto a floppy disk: Starting off with two blank disks, create a few dummy files and save them onto one of the disks, counting how many. Insert the other disk, create another file and initiate the process of saving up to the point where you have only to press one key to do it. By this point, the computer will have looked at the disk and found that it is blank. Now swap the disk again for the one with the test files on. If your computer saves the file onto this disk without losing, destroying or damaging any of the existing files, then it passes the test. If some of the files do disappear, then be warned – this is a bug that will get you sooner or later.

Of course, the answer is to keep a back up. But actually, if the tracks you have dumped to multitrack are all OK, then you don't really need that data on disk any more. All you need is the timecode start point and the tempo, plus any tempo changes and you can record new tracks without difficulty. After some disagreeable experiences with more than one sequencer I resolved always to write down these things, which takes about 10 seconds. I haven't lost a night's sleep since. If you use an external sync box, rather than a sequencer with an integrated SMPTE capability, you'll have to write down these things anyway.

The other problem that you will typically have to face is loss of timecode. Unfortunately, the timecode readers that sequencers have are sometimes not of the best. If they lose code for an instant they will probably grind to a halt. If the code on Track 16 becomes faulty, then the answer (at least one answer which doesn't require extra equipment) is to record fresh code onto another track. The start time will change so you'll have to determine this by trial and error, but it is surprisingly easy to do. End of problem.

Of course, the number of things that could potentially go wrong is limitless, but the two mentioned are the worst. Here are a few more minor difficulties:

• *The sequencer will not sync to the tape.*
The recording level of the timecode may be too high or too low. Set it to around -7dB to -5dB, or to the level the sequencer manufacturer suggests. Timecode should not be recorded with dbx noise reduction or with equalisation. And make sure the tape heads are clean!

The level of the timecode into the sequencer on playback may be incorrect. Experiment with the level until you find one that works reliably. It is possible to record timecode at a higher level on a digital recorder, but it may be too high for the sequencer or synchroniser on playback. Once again, experiment.

• *Sync is intermittent*
On an analogue multitrack, any bass instrument recorded on Track 15 will leak into Track 16 affecting the code. From time to time, or indeed perhaps all the time, this will make the code impossible to read. Erasing the track and recording at a lower level, or on another track, will usually cure this.

• *The sequencer will not sync during recording*
On an analogue multitrack this is probably due to crosstalk from Track 15 or even Track 14. Crosstalk in a combined record/playback head during recording is very high and may leak into the timecode. Use a lower recording level. It is possible to record timecode at a higher level on a digital recorder, but it may be too high for the sequencer or synchroniser on playback. Once again, experiment.

• *The sequence plays back at the wrong speed*
Some sequencers will automatically recognise the frame rate of the timecode and play at the correct speed. Others have to be set to the correct rate otherwise the tempo will be incorrect.

10 Compressor and noise gate

There is only one studio effect that is more useful than the compressor, so useful that it is nearly always incorporated into the mixing console itself – EQ. In fact, the next chapter is dedicated to EQ, but I think it's more important to talk about compression and gating first. Equalisation is nearly always necessary, but you can learn to apply EQ by instinct. Dynamic control is harder to get the hang of and use successfully, so while you are instinctively EQing, you can be applying some of the dynamics techniques I shall outline here.

Before looking at what a compressor does, and exploring the noise gate too, let's first of all consider why dynamic control is necessary in recording. After all, if we don't need compressors strapped to the sides of our heads, why do we need them when we record sound onto tape?

You had better give me a slap on the wrist for posing a trick question. The human ear does in fact have its own built in compression system. It's rather more compact than the units we normally mount in our nineteen inch racks, but it is nonetheless very effective. The ear basically consists of three sections which are prosaically called the outer ear, middle ear and inner ear respectively. The outer ear is basically that flap you have on the side of your head and the connecting passage down to the ear drum which picks up the sound. The inner ear is the transducer of the system converting vibrations, which are now travelling through fluid, into nerve impulses. There is a problem getting the sound vibrations from the eardrum into the fluid in the cochlea – the organ of the inner ear – because sound doesn't very much like to change from travelling in one medium to another. If there was no middle ear to make a correction, as much as 30 decibels of level would be wasted (this is apparently OK for some animals, but not for humans). The middle ear therefore has a mechanical amplifier consisting of three bones which act as levers, making up the loss. This is where the ear's compressor has its effect. When the incoming sound gets too loud, as it might if you go to a concert by the local gas board's pneumatic drill ensemble, a muscle around the three bones tightens and skews the levers reducing their efficiency, and therefore the level entering the inner ear. It's very clever and gives good protection against continuous loud sounds. (It's not so efficient at impulsive noises – evolution hasn't caught up yet with the drum machine. This reminds me of a joke: What do you call an old recording engineer who has listened to loud music for so long that his ears are completely shot to pieces? A producer!).

With the aid of its internal compressor, the ear can manage a pretty wide range of sounds. In quiet enough surroundings you can indeed hear a proverbial pin drop, and probably sounds even lower in level than that. At the other extreme, you probably wouldn't like to get too close to the take off runway at Heathrow Airport, but if you approached it gradually you would find that the noise was at first loud, then uncomfortably loud, and then painfully loud. Between the extremes of level from the quietest sound the ear can hear to the loudest the ear can handle there is a range of approximately 120dB.

It may come as a surprise in this age of technological marvels that few types of sound equipment can come even close to this. An analogue tape recorder can manage, on a good day, a dynamic range of about 65dB between its noise floor and the highest level it can record with acceptably low distortion. 16 bit digital equipment can in theory have a signal to noise ratio of 96dB. Even this is 24dB less than the ear's range. '24dB less' means that if you matched the volume so that the quietest sound your digital system could produce was the same as the quietest sound the ear could hear, then the loudest sound available from the digital system would be at a sound pressure level only one sixteenth of the ear's maximum level.

The upshot of all this is that any sound we want to record has to be squeezed through a system which has a much narrower dynamic range than the ear. The quietest sounds will need to be boosted if they are not going to be lost among low level noise, and the loudest sounds will need to be kept under control. This means that we need compression.

There is another aspect to dynamic range, apart from the fact that even modern equipment is not as 'hifi' as the ear. Do we actually need such a wide dynamic range when we play back a recording at home? If the loud parts of the music are too loud, then might not the neighbours become just a little fractious (and possibly litigious)? And if the

Fig 10.1 The Drawmer DL241 compressor with expander/gate

quiet parts are too quiet, will you still be able to hear them above the background noise inevitable in almost any domestic setting? The only answer is to control the dynamic range to make sure that it isn't too much, either for the equipment to handle or for the listening environment. This doesn't always mean using a compressor; sensible mixing and use of the faders is one of the best ways of making sure that the dynamic range of a recording is as you want it.

If one function of the compressor is to control dynamic range, then a completely separate function is its use as an effect. By 'effect' I mean changing a sound from its natural state into something intentionally different and artificial, either to improve it or simply make it more interesting. As will be seen later, the noise gate has 'corrective' and 'creative' uses too. And when we put the two together then we will really find out the power of dynamic control.

Using the compressor

One of the main uses of compression as an effect is recording vocals. Trained singers can sing at a consistent level and keep the difference

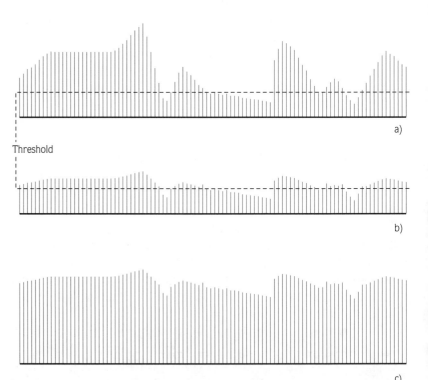

Fig 10.1 Compression and gain make up
a) Original signal
b) After compression
c) With gain make-up

between loud and soft passages within acceptable limits. Untrained singers usually don't have the same degree of breath control. Indeed, singing according to the rule book involves breathing from the diaphragm rather than the chest, and this does not form part of the vocal style of many of the most popular vocalists, so we need to compress. Figure 10.1a shows how the level of the vocal may vary widely, with a large dynamic range between the lowest the and highest levels. Compression is used to bring down the highest peaks, above the threshold level, leaving the lower levels just as they were, as in Figure 10.1b. Figure 10.1c shows the level restored so that the peaks are the same level as they were to start with, but the overall dynamic range is reduced. The result is a much more controlled sound.

Most compressors have pretty much the same controls:

Threshold sets the level where compression starts to take effect. Sounds below the threshold pass through unaltered and only sounds above the threshold are compressed.

Ratio sets the degree of compression above the threshold level. A ratio of 2:1 represents mild compression and means that when the incoming level (above the threshold) rises by 10dB, the outgoing level will only rise by 5dB. Ratios of up to 5:1 are regularly used for vocals and other instruments, and can pass by unnoticed by the listener if the other controls are set properly. Higher ratios are used for more serious limiting, where the level needs more severe control. Ratios of 10:1 and higher are nearly always noticeable to the listener.

Attack is measured in milliseconds and determines the time taken for the compressor to start working once the signal has passed the threshold level.

Release sets the length of time it takes for the compressor to return to its normal state once the signal has gone back below the threshold.

Gain is provided because compression always reduces the peak level: the more compression, the lower the level of the outgoing signal. This control is sometimes referred to as 'make-up' gain because it makes up the level that is inevitably lost during the compression process.

Of these five controls (there may be more on a more sophisticated device), Threshold, Ratio, Attack and Release are the most important. With these you can either improve a sound beyond all recognition or you can ruin it beyond salvation. I did say that the compressor was a powerful device. Thinking about vocals and single instruments for the moment, I usually decide what ratio to use just by listening, then I set it and start on the other controls. It's not the kind of procedure where you can set one control, fine tune it and then go on to the next. All the controls of the compressor seem to interact with each other and need careful balancing.

Having fairly arbitrarily set the ratio, I can go on to set the threshold level. This is where the important gain reduction meter on the compressor comes into play. The gain reduction meter tells you what the compressor is doing to the signal from moment to moment and gives you a visual check on what you are hearing. I usually like to hear a gain reduction of from 6 to 12dB. Above this much compression I can hear that the sound is being squeezed too much (although I may like it for an effect, as opposed to simply controlling the sound). Anything much below 6dB compression and you'll have a job hearing the difference.

An important point which often isn't mentioned is that at some occasions during the track, there should be no gain reduction (as indicated by the meter) at all. If the only time the meter reads zero dB gain reduction is when the instrument isn't playing, then when it does start you'll get a 'crack' as the compressor takes effect. Setting the threshold to a lower value normally gives more compression, but setting it to a lower value than necessary just gives you the undesirable side effects.

There is a balancing act between the Ratio and Threshold controls to give the right amount of compression, according to what your ears perceive, and there is also a balancing act between the Attack and Release controls and the signal, to reduce the potential obtrusiveness of the compressor. The principal reason why compressors have Attack and Release controls is so that you can make the compression come and go unnoticed. The settings have to be judged against the attack and decay envelope of the signal. Drums for example naturally have a fast attack and decay, so if the attack and release settings are too slow, the compression will not start quickly enough and the initial transient will get through uncompressed, and after the drum sound has gone you will hear the compressor gradually reducing the amount of gain reduction as it returns to normal. This last effect is known as 'breathing' or 'pumping', and occurs when you can hear background noise changing in level unmasked by the signal. If the Attack and Release controls are set properly, the signal should hide any level changes in the background. The best way to set attack and release is to match the attack and decay characteristics of the signal itself. That way you won't get more pumping than necessary.

Having said how to set the attack and release times correctly, let's explore how they can be set incorrectly, but to good effect. One use of the compressor is to make drum sounds more punchy. This is done, just as I mentioned above, by setting a slow attack. The initial transient of the drum then gets through before the compressor clamps down on the remainder of the waveform. Figure 10.2 shows what happens. This is a very useful technique for guitars as well. Curiously enough, the compressor is actually working to expand the dynamic range around the time of the initial transient. What a strange world! The Release control, as well as having an effect on how much pumping you will hear, can also change the amount of compression going on. In fact the Release control has as much effect on that as have the Ratio and Threshold controls.

Let me give an example: I went to an audio exhibition several years ago where a friendly American was demonstrating a compressor – the best compressor in the world, needless to say. "That's 30dB compression", he was saying, which is the same as saying 30dB gain reduction, which is a lot, "Can you hear it working?". I had to admit that I couldn't hear any pumping at all, nor could I hear the characteristic 'compressor' sound which you would certainly expect from a unit working that hard. I looked a little closer at the gain reduction meter. It was right at the end of the scale as I expected, but more importantly it wasn't moving. This is a crucial point about compression. Unless the gain reduction meter is moving then no compression is taking place. The demonstrator had craftily set a very long release time and virtually all that the compressor was doing was lowering the gain on a steady state basis. To get any use out of the compressor, not only do you have to see the LEDs of the gain reduction meter light up, you also have to see them move. The faster they move up and down, the more effective compression you are getting. (And the more you are likely to hear pumping).

The other important control you will always find on a compressor is the Stereo Link switch. This is quickly explained: If you are compressing a stereo signal, the levels in the two channels will be unequal and will change from moment to moment. Unless something is done the amount of compression will be different in the two channels, making the stereo image shift from one speaker to the other according to which channel is being compressed the most. To avoid this, the Stereo Link switch mixes the control signals for the gain elements together so that each channel is compressed to the same extent.

The noise gate

The noise gate is the counterpart to the compressor. If you have a compressor, then you had better have a gate too. Compressing any signal reduces its dynamic range, so therefore any noise content is closer to the level of the signal peaks than it was before compression. In other words, compression reduces the signal to noise ratio. This is

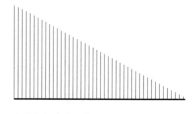

a) Original signal

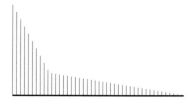

b) After compression – initial transient gets through

Fig 10.2 A drum sound processed by a compressor with a slow attack time

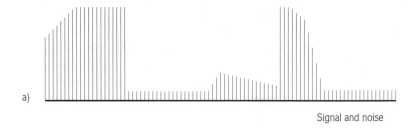

a)

Signal and noise

b)

Clean signal

Fig 10.3 Removing unwanted noise

inevitable. If you are compressing a mixed signal, whether mono or stereo, then you have to put up with this or use an expander to try and help matters. Expanders are not all that commonplace so I'll leave them for you to discover for yourself. Noise gates however are commonplace, ubiquitous in fact, and they are very useful for getting rid of noise on single instruments, as you find in multitrack recording. Figure 10.3a shows a signal with a certain amount of noise content. If the signal had been compressed, then the noise level would have been higher. As you can see, while the instrument is playing, it masks the noise completely. The noise is still present, but the ear doesn't notice it. If we can close off the channel – or 'gate' it – when the instrument isn't playing, then we won't hear the noise at all and end up with something like Figure 10.3b – a nice clean signal. If you haven't heard noise gating, it's amazing what an effect it has, but remember that it only works where there are gaps in the signal that can be totally silenced.

Noise gates have similar controls to compressors:

Threshold sets the level below which the signal will be cut off completely.
Attack and *Release* have precisely the same meaning as in the compressor.
Hold sets the length of time the gate will remain fully open after a signal has descended below the threshold.
Range sets the degree of attenuation when the gate is closed.

Stereo link works in pretty much the same way as in the compressor.

Setting the noise gate can be tricky. The first control to go for is the Threshold where you decide which parts of the signal you want to keep and which you want to lose. The Attack control sets how quickly the gate will open, and should be set to match the attack time of the instrument you are gating. Too fast an attack (less then 1 millisecond) may cause a click at the beginning of each sound. The hold and release times can be tricky to set. What you want is for the gate to close as soon as the signal has died away, but not reopen during the signal's decay. An incorrect setting of hold and release can cause 'jitter' where the gate opens and closes several times while the signal is diminishing — it sounds dreadful and can only be cured by matching the release profile of the gate to the decay of the signal, and also getting the threshold spot on. Some gates make it easier by having a Trigger Mask control, which sets a length of time from the initial opening of the gate during which it will not open again. In my opinion, all gates should have a Trigger Mask because it not only makes it much easier to set the gate up, it makes it possible to get a much greater variety of effects from the Hold and Release controls.

Effects

When you bring the compressor and gate together you can get an enormous range of effects, especially on drum sounds, although the combination is useful for guitars as well. You can make drums more punchy, make the sounds longer or shorter, apply gated reverb in the way you want rather than the way some digital effects unit manufacturer has decided you must have it.

When you try it, you'll find there are a lot of possibilities. I have tried to show a few of these in diagrammatic form (Figure 10.4). The original sound has a fairly slow decay which can be created by adding a bit of reverb before passing the sound through the compressor. If the diagrams look tempting, wait till you hear the results.

There's so much more to say about compressors and gates that it would take an encyclopaedia to fit it all in. There's more on the subject in following chapters.

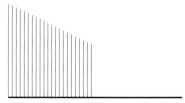

Original signal

Envelope shortened with smooth decay

Fast decay

Slow attack

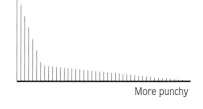

More punchy

Fig 10.4 Examples of how a sound's dynamic characteristics can be changed with a compressor and noise gate

Punchy and very tight

11 Equalisation

L anguage is such a funny thing that I sometimes wonder how we manage to communicate at all. For instance, according to a learned volume on my bookshelf, the word 'nice' didn't used to mean nice at all. It used to mean 'precise'. Similarly, 'quite' didn't mean 'almost', it meant 'absolutely'! 'Equalisation' is a word my book doesn't mention, but when used in the context of making recordings one might wonder what on earth are we meant to be making equal, and equal to what? The answer to this question, and to many other of life's great mysteries is... historical reasons.

Before mixing consoles were invented, indeed before any form of recording other than direct to 78 rpm shellac disc was invented, telephone engineers were working on a problem concerning the sound quality of their lines. As you might expect if you send a telephone signal down a very long cable, some of the sound gets lost. (As a matter of interest, the first transatlantic cable was laid well before the beginning of this century and therefore before recording of any kind). But different frequencies are lost in different amounts according to the characteristics of the cable. This means that the signal coming out the far end of the cable is not the same as the signal that went in, either in level or frequency balance. In other words it is unequal to it. So what the telephone engineers came up with was a process called equalisation, using circuitry which changes the balance of frequencies of the signal. Today we use similar processes to change the frequency balance of our musical signals, and so we use the same term – equalisation, or EQ for short.

If you look at the circuitry of any equaliser, you will see the same types of components: The capacitor is a component which passes higher frequencies easily while making it difficult for low frequencies to get through. The inductor works in the reverse manner, letting low frequencies pass through. (Clever circuitry can allow capacitors, which are easier to obtain in precise values, to simulate the effects of inductors). Variable and fixed value resistors control how much of the signal is allowed to pass along any signal path, for example through a capacitor to earth where it will be taken to that great last resting place of audio signals everywhere.

As well as these three passive components, small amplifiers are used to accentuate the effects of the frequency-sensitive components and to make up signal losses. Analogue audio equalisers consist of these four types of component only, but designers have come up with different ways of making them useful to the operator. The three main types of equaliser you will come across are mixing console EQ, graphic EQ and parametric EQ. There are some other weird and wonderful devices which operate in ways of their own, but still use the same four basic types of component internally.

Console EQ

I mentioned console EQ earlier in Chapter 5, but now is the time to go into a bit more detail. This is an area where designers and manufacturers seriously need to look at their products and ask themselves whether they are doing as well as they could be. Some are most definitely not. To get subjective for a moment there are two types of EQ, which may look exactly the same from the operator's point of view but sound totally different.

I would like to make an analogy with woodworking to make my point clear: The chisel is a very useful tool for removing precise quantities of wood for making simple slots or complex joints. A sharp chisel is a pleasure to use, just position it correctly, give it exactly the right amount of force and it will fashion the wood almost as though you were doing it by mind power alone. A blunt chisel is completely the opposite, it will do the work, but grudgingly and with a poor end result. A good EQ – and I don't necessarily mean a complicated EQ – will shape the sound just the way you want it, precisely and with positive effect. A poor or mediocre EQ will have an effect, but it's unlikely to achieve what you want it to. Advertisements may claim 'smooth, musical equalisation' or similar, but don't believe anything other than your own ears. I must add at this point that there still isn't any consensus on what actually makes a good EQ, apart from the fact that you know it when you hear it. Most engineers who have any knowledge of what goes on inside an equaliser will have their opinions, and I'll be passing on mine, but there is plenty of scope for some solid research to be done to find out exactly what makes a good equaliser tick.

The most basic form of EQ is the filter. Figure 11.1 shows the various effects filters can have on a flat signal. There are two basic types of filter: high pass and low pass. Everyone finds these terms confusing because a high pass filter cuts out low frequencies and a low pass filter cuts out high frequencies, so the name of the filter is opposite to the range of frequencies where it has its effect. There is a third type, the bandpass filter which is a combination of high and low pass in series. Both principal types of filter have two main parameters: cut-off frequency and slope. The cut-off frequency of a filter is

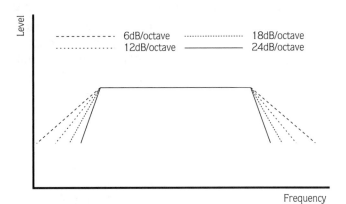

Fig 11.1 High pass and low pass filter responses

defined as the frequency at which the level is 3 decibels below the pass band level. The slope is the maximum rate at which the level drops off above or below the cut-off frequency. Slopes nearly always come in multiples of six: 6dB/octave, 12dB/octave, 18dB/octave and 24dB/octave. This is because filters are very easy to make with these slopes, very difficult with in-between values (and with slopes greater than 24dB/octave). A 6dB/octave filter can be made with just two passive components and has a very smooth roll off. At the other extreme, a 24dB/octave filter has a strong effect and really does things to the sound. Given the choice, I would like to have variable frequency 24dB/octave high and low pass filters in the EQ section of my console because they would give me the power I need, and I would like to think I am able to use that power sensibly. You can't go wrong with a 6dB/octave filter, or even 12dB/octave, but you can't really do all that much either.

The high and low frequency EQ controls, which are separate from the filters, are very important too. The two types you are likely to find are shown in Figure 11.2. The bell curve cuts or boosts a range of frequencies around its centre point, the shelf cuts or boosts all frequencies above or below the stated frequency. (In practice, the shelf will roll off so that frequencies at the very edges of the audio band and beyond are not boosted unnecessarily). Both of these curves have their uses, and upmarket consoles will provide a switch to give you the choice.

When it comes to actually using the high and low frequency EQ controls, you will find that there can be an immense difference between the EQ on different consoles, even when the controls look and are labelled the same. I don't mean that the more complex facilities of upmarket consoles necessarily provide any extra benefit in themselves, what I am talking about is the difference between the sharp chisel and the blunt chisel. It's possible to have a sophisticated EQ that's not very impressive, and a simple EQ that sounds great.

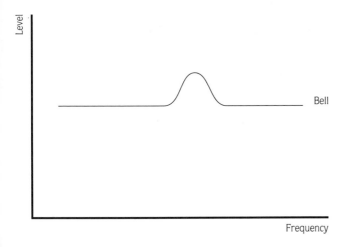

Bell

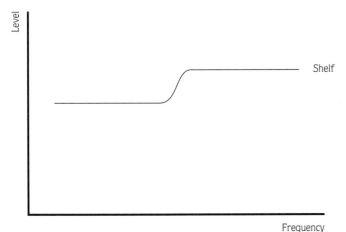

Shelf

Fig 11.2 High frequency EQ responses

The mid frequency EQ sections on most consoles sound a lot more similar to each other than do the high and low frequency controls, so I'll refer you to the section that follows later on parametric EQ. The mid frequency controls on most consoles are simple parametrics without the Q control.

Graphic EQ

Graphics are a great invention, there's no doubt about that. But there is also no doubt that the graphic isn't an answer to all EQ needs. The reason graphics came into being is that it's fairly simple to design a variable-gain bandpass filter section, therefore it's not a long train of thought that takes you to the idea that it might be nice to have a whole load of them to adjust different frequency bands covering the audio range. Add linear controls rather than rotary knobs and the graphic is born.

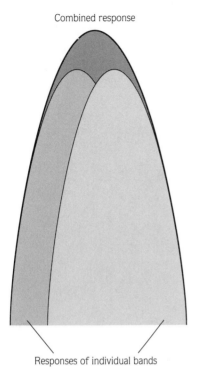

Combined response

Responses of individual bands

Fig 11. 3 Combining adjacent graphic EQ bands

A typical graphic equaliser will have around thirty bands to cover the full range from 20Hz to 20kHz. Some graphics have less, but they are not nearly as useful. Graphic equalisers may be described as being '1/3 octave' graphics. This means that each band covers a frequency range which is simply a third of an octave, and you can cut or boost all frequencies in that band by up to 12 or 18dB. In reality, the response of each band extends outside its stated range, simply because it's impossible to have a filter with infinitely steep slopes. It probably wouldn't sound too brilliant either. This is where the 'graphic' concept falls down. It's easy to believe that, because you have sliders running up and down showing the level of each band in the vertical direction and the frequency of the bands horizontally, the slider knobs trace out a graph of the frequency response. They don't. They do give a rough guide but, for instance, if two adjacent sliders were set to +6dB, then the degree of boost at frequencies in between would be rather more than this.

Figure 11.3 shows what happens. This of course isn't a problem as long as you are aware of it. Graphic equalisers are great for picking out problem frequencies or ranges of frequencies and dealing with them. As I shall explain later, they are also good for shaping the response over the whole frequency range. As far as changing the sound of individual instruments is concerned however, they are blunt chisels.

Parametric EQ

Parametric EQ is so called because nobody could think of a better name for it. At least that's my theory. I suppose that at the time it was invented it offered control over more of the parameters of the signal than any other EQ so it was as good a name as any. Parametric equalisers have three controls for each frequency band and a typical unit will have perhaps five bands altogether. The three controls are Frequency, Gain and Q. The 'Q' control is sometimes called bandwidth – the knob does exactly the same thing. Figure 11.4 shows the effects of the controls. The Frequency control sets the centre frequency around which the boost, or cut, will take place. Gain sets the amount of cut or boost at the centre frequency. Q sets the sharpness of the bell shaped curve.

Doubtless there will be recording engineers who will be content just to use the Q control without understanding how the values are worked out, but since you're taking the trouble to read up on the subject here is the story of Q (no relation to James Bond's gadget supplier).

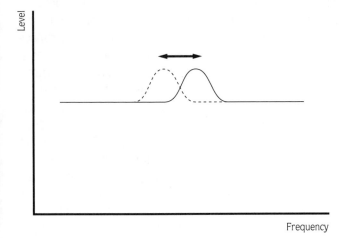

(a) Frequency

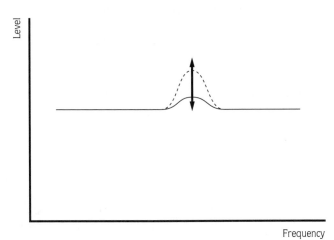

(b) Gain

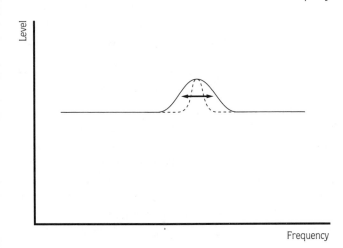

(c) Q

Fig 11.4 The effect of varying the three standard parametric EQ controls

In the early days of radio, circuit designers were trying to produce a device which would react strongly to the signal from one radio station and reject signals from others. Circuits were built using capacitors and inductors (exactly the same components found in equalisers), and some were found to be better than others. A radio station transmits its signal on a very narrow band of frequencies and the more precise the response of the detector, the more it will react to those frequencies. By reducing the resistance of the coil, engineers found that the sharpness of the response, or the sharpness of resonance as they would say, improved. To compare different circuits, it was necessary to measure this sharpness, referred to as Q (after Quality of resonance, some people say). It was decided that Q would be defined by the value of the centre frequency divided by the arithmetical difference between the two frequencies where the response had dropped by 3dB. Q can be measured in other ways, but they all amount to the same thing.

For audio purposes, Q is the centre frequency divided by the bandwidth between the -3dB points and it is just a simple ratio, it has no units. 'Bandwidth', as you can see from the last sentence, refers to the range of frequencies between the two points where the level is 3dB down from the level at the centre frequency. On an equaliser, it would be measured in octaves or fractions of an octave.

Using EQ

Let's be clear on one thing: You don't have to use EQ. If the sound you are recording is good with no equalisation, then you don't have to put any in just because it's there. But there may be problems with the sound that EQ can correct, or EQ can be used to enhance a sound and make it better than real life. I'll examine the corrective aspects of EQ first.

If you're making a live recording then there will be no shortage of unwanted noise. Some of it you'll just have to live with (like on one occasion I had to live with the helicopters fluttering around the church where I was recording a concert of 13th century music). Other noises can be reduced by EQ or filtering. There is very often a problem with excess bass in live work, simply because bass frequencies find it easier to propagate in large auditoria. If microphones are suspended on wires or ropes, then they may be subject to convection currents in the air which will generate low frequency noise, sometimes so low you can't hear it but you see the meters dancing up and down and wonder what's going on.

Another source of low frequency noise is the stand mounted

microphone on a wooden stage. Foot noise works its way up the stand and into the mic no matter how well it is suspended. The solution is to flick the mixing console's high pass filter into circuit (remembering that 'high pass' means 'low cut'). If you have a choice of frequencies, 80 or 90Hz is good and unnoticeable, 150Hz combats stronger low frequency noise but does remove some bass. I am always inclined to use the high pass filter on any instrument that doesn't produce any bass, just leaving it out for male vocalists with deep voices, bass guitars, double basses etc.

Coming back into the studio, every so often someone is going to bring you a tape with mains hum on it and ask you to fix it. Mains hum has a habit of creeping into the most orderly of recording setups. In a fixed installation it can normally be dealt with, but elsewhere it can be a problem and it is often not spotted until after the event (which is why you have to deal with it now in the studio). Fortunately, the graphic equaliser will be able to help. It can't cure the problem, but if you remember that mains hum has a frequency of 50Hz in the UK, and that it will have harmonics at 100Hz and 150Hz etc, then you can reduce its effects simply by pulling down the sliders closest to those frequencies. The program material will sound hardly any different.

Equalisation has countless creative uses. As I said before, you don't have to use it if the sound is OK to start with, but well used EQ can make the difference between a rough amateurish recording and slick professionalism. The first creative use of EQ is to improve the basic sounds of instruments which you may, if you wish, do as you record them onto multitrack tape. Console EQ and parametrics are best for this purpose. We'll save the graphics for later. If you are EQing an instrument as you are recording it, then you'll be doing one of two things. You will either be enhancing the instrument while still retaining its characteristics, or you'll be EQing so heavily that you are producing a new sound entirely. In the second case, go ahead and EQ as much as you like because you are using your own artistic judgment which needs no advice from anyone else. But if you are simply enhancing a sound it's important to be careful. Usually you will want to bring out an instrument's essential characteristics and reduce any undesirable by-products. Do this sparingly and you will make overdubs and mixing easier and more pleasant. But overdo it and you'll make life more difficult later on. Remember that what you take away, you can't always put back.

During the mix, EQ is used to make the various sounds blend together well. You can mix for clarity or for 'thickness'. I'll explain in more detail when I come to the subject of mixdown later in Chapter 14, but basically you can mix for clarity by finding the characteristic

A more offensive form of mains hum is dimmer noise, produced by thyristor controlled lighting dimmers close to audio equipment and cables. This too has a fundamental frequency of 50Hz, but it has harmonics all the way up the audio band and beyond. Conventional graphic EQ can make things slightly better, but don't hope for miracles.

The graphic equaliser is useful when you are mixing, to shape the overall sound. Plug the console's stereo output into the graphic and go through that onto tape (remembering to make sure that you are monitoring the output of the graphic – you'll do this in different ways on different consoles). Once again, I'll explain more when I cover mixdown itself in Chapter 14, but for now just let me say that using a graphic in this way gives you an opportunity to colour the sound in a way that can't be achieved using the console EQ on a channel-by-channel basis.

105

frequency range of each instrument and lifting it a little. Also reduce the frequencies where each instrument doesn't contribute very much. This will produce a mix where the instruments stand out from each other. To mix for thickness, reduce the level of each instrument's characteristic frequency range slightly, This will help instruments blend together. Usually, if you are working with 'real' instruments then you will be trying to get more clarity. If you are working with synthesised sounds then they are probably too clear to start with.

With EQ, it all comes down in the end to using your ears and if it sounds good (and if you can rely on your monitor speakers to give you the true picture) then it is good. Don't use too much, think about what you are doing and why you are doing it and the various types of equaliser will become your indispensable companions in your voyage through the wonderful world of recording techniques.

Effects 12

Just as variety is the spice of life, the effects rack can have the same effect on your music as the spice rack in the kitchen – helping the flavours of the instrumental and vocal sounds to blend together, or to add a bit of fire into your productions! We have so many types of effects at our disposal these days that it's almost confusing, and a time consuming process to choose the preset that adds that special 'something' to a musical line. But when there's so much on offer from the various manufacturers, it's probably a good idea to step back and take in a perspective on what the basic effects are, why they were invented and what they can do. Developing your own combination of effects from basic ingredients is analogous to the chef who will carefully select from his range of herbs and spices, rather than casually throwing in a handful of curry powder. But where to start? Let's go back in time to a point when recording techniques were so primitive that there were no effects and ask the question: Why do some of those early recordings still sound so good?

The one effect that has been around almost since the beginning of recording is compression, which I dealt with in detail in Chapter 10. In fact, compression didn't start as an effect as such, it came about as a dire necessity to compress the dynamic range of real life into the restrictions imposed by early recording media. It was only later that compression was used as a true effect to enhance sounds, rather than smooth away problems. The same applies to equalisation, which was invented to ameliorate shortcomings in the frequency response of equipment, and then found favour as a way of adjusting the frequency balance of a sound or a mix. Before the 1960s, engineers just didn't have a need for effects like we do now. The men in white coats didn't go around saying things like, 'Bing's voice could do with a touch of PCM70'. They had enough problems getting the sound clearly onto the tape in the first place without messing around with it further. If you like, you could say that the equipment itself produced all the effects you might ever need: EQ produced by resonances in the microphone, compression and distortion by the tape recording process (and by all the valves in the equipment), reverberation and echo by print through in the tape, and time domain effects in the wow and flutter produced by the motors and bearings in tape recorders, cutting lathes and record players.

Ironically, as the performance of the equipment got better and better, the more we needed effects to thicken up the sound, right up to modern times where synths and samplers send an ultra clean signal directly along a piece of wire through a mixing console which approaches the limits of what is technically possible, onto an almost noise-free digital tape recorder. With equipment this clean, we need a whole rack full of effects units to dirty up the sound and get back to square one. Is this progress? Well of course it is, because now we can dictate the way we want things to sound, rather than have to put up with conditions imposed by less-than-perfect equipment. The reason that some early recordings sound very good is because musicians and engineers adapted their styles and their techniques to the circumstances in which they found themselves, in much the same way as the unrealistic sound of a sampler transposing a real instrument up or down in pitch has been widely exploited as a musical device in its own right.

Reverb

Reverberation is a natural phenomenon that can improve the quality of even the weakest singers. We all know how pleasurable it can be to sing in the bath because the high level of reflected sound adds a full-ness and roundness to the sound that in reality may be totally absent. It's not convenient, or desirable, to set up a recording studio in a bathroom – you wouldn't want to slip on the soap – so it's better to have some kind of artificial way of generating reverberation, or reverb as it has come to be called.

Since a room with hard tiled surfaces produces a lot of reflections, leading to reverberation, studios hit on the idea of building an echo chamber, probably in the basement. An echo chamber is a room with a loudspeaker, one or two microphones and lots of irregular hard sur-faces. Sound is piped down from the mixing console through a power amp into the speaker, picked up by the mics (which are angled away from the speaker) and put back into the mix. It's an obvious thing to do when you think about it. In actual fact, the sound produced by a real echo chamber isn't all that brilliant, mainly because small rooms have strong resonances which colour the sound too much. Nevertheless, it was a lot better than nothing and real echo chamber reverb has been used on lots of recordings. There is one interesting point about echo chambers that is still relevant – the feed to the chamber need only be mono with one speaker. If there are two mics, they will each pick up slightly different combinations of reflections giving an entirely adequate stereo effect. The benefits of having a stereo send to an echo chamber, or modern effects unit, are sonically so slight as to be negligible.

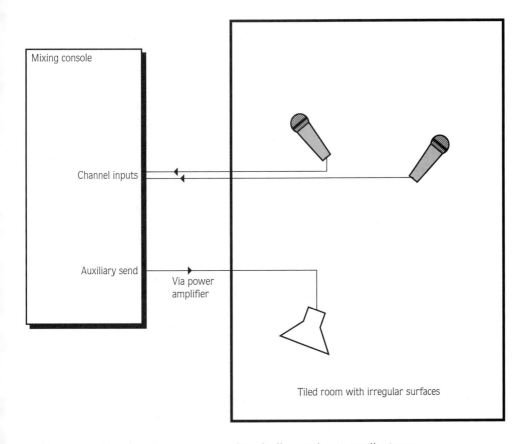

Fig 12.1 Echo chamber

Because echo chambers were rather bulky and not easily trans-portable (!), various mechanical solutions were tried. The two that were found to work best were the spring and plate. Spring reverbs have been awarded a high degree of notoriety, basically because most examples of the type sound truly awful. Even at their highest state of development, for example in a number of products by AKG, no-one could put their hand on their heart and say that they produced the perfect reverb. A spring reverb works by having a loudspeaker-like transducer impart a mechanical vibration into a long spring. This vibration rushes to the end of the spring, bounces back and forward and generally gets very confused. The sound that is picked up and transformed back into electricity has a lot of the qualities you would like reverb to have – plus some qualities that you wouldn't wish upon your worst enemy. Spring reverbs, to put it bluntly, twang. Well, you would expect it I suppose. Percussive sounds and spring reverbs just do not go together because you get that horrible twanging sound on every beat.

The one spring reverb that you are likely to come across second-hand these days is the Great British Spring. I had one myself when digital reverbs were fantastically expensive (and still not all that much good). The good point about the Great British Spring was that the sound was very dense and really gave a good thickening quality to sustained synth voices. Even now, a digital reverb can be judged by how much thickening power it provides.

If spring reverbs have never been up to much, the other mechanical reverb is a different kettle of fish (no – not literally). The plate reverb really does give a good clean, smooth, thick sound. A plate made by EMT is still something to have in the studio, alongside current devices. The plate works in much the same way as a spring, by having one transducer make the plate vibrate and another two to pick up the stereo reverb. If I had room for one, and a few pennies to spare, I would definitely be looking for an echo plate for my own use because I think they have a sound quality that will always be valuable.

Digital reverbs offer so much convenience that they are found everywhere. Someone will probably even make a digital reverb for use in the bathroom one day. There is a lot of difference between different units, and it's something that you can't really find out about by looking at spec sheets, you have to listen. On any unit there will be a variety of programs to simulate different environments such as small rooms, medium size rooms, halls and cathedrals. The essential difference between each program is the pattern of reflections and you are not usually given much control over this. Within each program are a number of parameters. Reverb time is simply the time taken for the level to drop from its maximum by 60 decibels. High frequency damping cuts down high frequencies more and more as the sound decays. This simulates a room with wall surfaces that absorb high frequencies more than low. Pre-delay is a time period inserted before the signal is fed to the effects circuitry. Having a slight gap between the clean signal and the reverb can help to maintain clarity while making a sound more dense.

Delay

Going back to basics once again, the original source of delay was the good old analogue tape recorder. Studios would keep a trusty old Revox A77 specially for this purpose loaded up with a reel of long play tape. Delay was added by sending the signal via an auxiliary to the tape recorder and bringing it back to a spare channel. Repeat echo could be obtained by sending some of that signal via the aux back to the Revox, thus creating a feedback loop. This technique was extensively used by Jamaican 'dub' producers who would ride the echo fader through the song and occasionally push it up into positive feedback where the echo would get higher and higher in level and eventually crack up in distortion. Not everybody's cup of ganja perhaps but it found a market. The big drawback to working with a tape recorder was that the tape had a habit of running out every half and hour or so, depending on what varispeed setting you had used. I used to have a craving for stereo echo, so I would find myself jumping up and down like a yoyo during a lengthy mix session just to take care of this. Mega boring!

The invention of digital delays provided an answer to this problem, and of course now that it's so easy, the effect is going out of fashion! But even if you hardly hear an echo these days, it doesn't mean that you can't use it at a subliminal level to improve your mix. Now, delay is incorporated into multieffects units with a number of useful parameters: Delay Time is obviously the time taken from the original signal to the repeat. It would be useful if all delay units would give the option of reading the delay time in beats per minute because that would help the engineer find a musically useful setting, rather than having to work out the number of milliseconds on a calculator (more on this in Chapter 13).

Feedback is used within the unit to give repeat echoes, rather than going through the desk. To simulate the softening effect of multiple repeats through an analogue tape machine, most delay units – or delay programs on multieffects units – have a high frequency damping setting, which filters the signal a little on each pass around the feedback loop. What digital delays don't yet have, and probably never will, is a setting to make them sound exactly like old analogue tape delay, which just goes to show that you can rarely completely replace a piece of gear with something more modern that can almost – but not entirely – do the same thing.

Time domain effects

Time domain effects include chorusing, phasing and flanging, all subtly different varieties of the same thing. To explain chorusing, we need to look at Figure 12..2. This could be done using an extra tape recorder with varispeed, which makes it easier to explain than trying to imagine what goes on inside a digital black box. As shown, the tape recorder will produce a single echo and nothing more, which will thicken the sound up a little. But when you apply your musically trained fingertips to the varispeed control, you will find that when you increase the speed, the pitch of the echo will rise. When you decrease the speed, the pitch will fall. Note that this only happens when the speed is changing, not when you leave it at the faster or

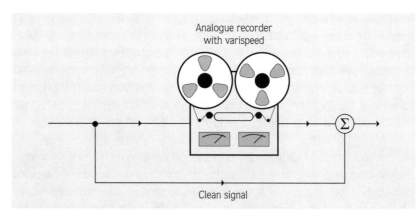

Fig 12.2 Chorusing with a 3-head tape recorder

slower setting. So you have continuously to shift the varispeed knob up and down, which might be a little tedious, but you will find that the sound is miraculously transformed from a thin and weedy vocal (probably) to something with depth and body. If you could do this with two varispeed tape recorders out of sync the result would be twice as good and you could pan the resulting stereo signal left and right. Isn't it great that we can get all of this in a rack mounting box these days?

The terms phasing and flanging have changed their meanings somewhat over the years, but there are two separate effects here so I'll describe both and let lexicographers argue about the terminology.

Figure 12.3 shows a multitrack tape recorder with both sync and replay heads, together with a quarter inch recorder for delay. The main signal for mixdown comes from the replay head, but if a separate sync output is available from the record head, as it would be in a pro recorder, then an output can be taken which is in advance of the replay output. This is fed to the delay recorder which is varispeeded so that the delay is exactly the same as the delay between the sync and replay heads on the multitrack. Both these signals are mixed together in the console. If the delay is exact, then in theory the signals will reinforce each other and simply become 6 decibels louder. But if the delay is slightly out, then an effect known as comb filtering

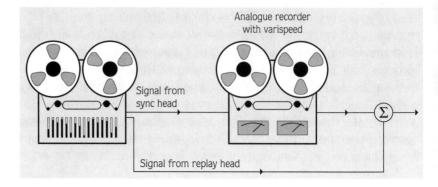

Fig 12.3 Using a multitrack recorder, plus a second recorder for delay, to produce a flanging effect

occurs which reinforces some frequencies while cancelling others out almost completely. This doesn't sound very good as a steady state effect, but when you shift the varispeed up and down, as before, then the sound becomes very rich, lively and interesting.

Another way of shifting the delay, rather more crude than using a varispeed control is by pressing the flange of the supply reel of the delay recorder – hence the term 'flanging'. These days, we would more likely think of the effect as being 'phasing' because of the phase cancellations that occur, and save the term 'flanging' for when positive feedback is added to make the effect stronger. Just like chorusing, phasing and flanging processes have been digitised and incorporated into multieffects units.

Aural exciter and pitch changer

The original Aural Exciter was made by the Aphex company and was considered to be so wonderful that studios couldn't buy it, they had to lease it by the track-minute! Exciters, in general, work by adding a controlled amount of distortion to the signal. OK, so you might be able to distort the signal in a thousand ways from microphone to loudspeaker, but not like this. The secret is to compress heavily the signal before passing it through the distortion producing circuitry, and then add this almost constant amount of 'fizz' to the clean signal. It may sound crazy, but the fact is that it works. Especially on material that is lacking in high frequencies, the exciter can add more brightness than any EQ HF control.

The last effect on my list is the pitch changer, or Harmonizer as it was called by its inventor, the Eventide company. The pitch changer exists only in the digital domain as there is no mechanical or electronic means of doing this job effectively (I'm told that a pitch changing tape recorder with a rotating head did not work too well, and I'm not surprised).

Pitch changing can never be performed perfectly, at least not at the current state of the art, and some devices will cope better with certain sounds than others. The prime use for pitch changing is for thickening up vocals by adding small amounts of signal a small fraction of a semitone up or down from the normal signal. This produces an effect similar to chorusing, but without the cyclic up and down motion. For novelty effects, delayed feedback of a pitch changed signal is great. If you have never heard the effect of a repeat echo that changes in pitch on every repeat, then you owe it to yourself to try it out. It's not for every day usage but who says that serious engineers can't have a bit of fun now and then?

Another time domain effect which has mechanical origins can be traced back to the Leslie loudspeaker. The Leslie speaker basically has two horns from which the sound emerges, and these horns rotate. At any time, one horn will be approaching the listener and one will be receding. In the same manner as the two-tone siren of a police car seems to fall in pitch as the car goes past (due to the Doppler effect), the sound from the horn which is coming towards you will be raised in pitch and the pitch of the sound from the receding horn will fall. This rise and fall in pitch isn't constant but varies with the angle between the listener and the mouth of the horn. In theory, this should give an effect similar to chorusing, but reality is quite different and I don't think there is anything on the digital market that can rival the true sound of a Leslie in the flesh. But there will be, one day.

Yamaha invented multi-effects and their SPX models can be found in almost every studio

One of the problems with effects, these days, is that multieffects make it so easy to try one effects combination after another, probably saying 'No... not quite.. almost... I don't like that...', and on ad infinitum.

I use a Yamaha SPX 90 and a pair of Alesis Quadraverb 2's and I'm well pleased with what they can do – even if they are not current state of the art – but there are times when I just want to go back to basics, so I plug my Fender Stratocaster guitar into a spare Alesis Microverb, which makes a great high impedance guitar preamp with the reverb turned right down. I take this to my Drawmer DL221 compressor to add some bite to the signal which then passes to a Fender Champ practice amp (the output of which is cut down from 6 watts to 1.5 by a series parallel resistor network to turn some of the sound into heat rather than make a lot of noise). The highly distorted guitar sound that emerges then goes to a Chorus program on the SPX 90 multieffects unit, and then through a Drawmer DS201 gate to get rid of the noise that has by now built up. A bit of EQ on the console and the sound is... I almost said perfect, but the point I want to make is that it can be a lot more fun to build up an effect than just to select a favourite preset on the multieffects unit. Effects provide a way to make your sound different from everyone else's, so go to it, be creative and let effects add spice to your musical life.

The mix | 13

That phrase, 'We'll fix it in the mix', has hopefully become part of recording history now that everyone has well and truly learned that whatever is wrong on the multitrack is going to be wrong on the final stereo mixdown. And if there is a mistake to be covered up, it's going to take ten times as long to fix it at the mixing stage than it would to correct during track laying. Mixing a multitrack tape into stereo is definitely an art. There is very little 'technique' to it because every move you make is governed by what you hear coming out of the monitor speakers, and the rule is 'if it sounds good, do it', and that shall be the whole of the law. Having said that, I also have to say that you really need to be sure that what sounds good to you is also going to sound good to all the potential purchasers of your record or CD, or listeners on their car stereos, but the number one item on the agenda during any mixing session is the need to get the message of the music across to the listener. Whatever form that message takes from 'eat your greens and save the planet' to simply 'get up and dance', this is the point where it could all come together or all fall apart.

The first thing you need for a successful mixing session is a well recorded multitrack tape. If this has been prepared properly, then mixing will be a smooth painless process. But if there are problems to be ironed out, then you'll spend much of your energy coping with these, leaving less to spare on creating a good mix. The worst situation you could find yourself in is being asked to mix a tape which has been badly recorded by someone else. If you are lucky enough to have some kind of automation to help you out then things might not be so bad. But if you have to fix problems and make a good mix at the same time by pure finger power, then jolly good luck to you. I've been there myself and I don't like it.

The one thing I can't do in a book like this, unfortunately, is tell you how to mix because the only way to learn is by experience, but I can pass on a few ideas which will help a budding recording engineer get a better sound, and get it more quickly. I'm going to assume that there is no automation on the console and everything is done by hand. Automation isn't by any means common yet, apart from at the high end of the business where it is almost ubiquitous. One day we'll all have it, but for now we need to have our fingers at the ready. Let's roll the tape...

The perfect tape

There's no such thing as the perfect multitrack recording, all ready and waiting to be mixed down with no EQ, level changes, effects and jiggery-pokery of various kinds. But it would be nice if we could direct our efforts towards making the raw material of the mix as easy to deal with as possible. Let's see what the requirements are:

If the recording is of a band using 'real' instruments, then there is probably a lot of extraneous noise on the tape that you could really have done without. As I said earlier, the time to deal with problems is during the session. If, for instance, the guitarist hits a string accidentally at a time when he is not supposed to be playing; don't leave the noise in – erase it. The time to erase it is while the player is still strapped into his instrument and plugged into his amp so if by some foul stroke of luck you erase something that should have been kept, it can be done again. This is sometimes a question of judgment because there may be a sound you don't want on the tape next to something that the player only got right by the most incredible stroke of good fortune. If this is the case then don't take chances, but always keep in mind that the cleaner you keep the tape during track laying, the easier the mix will be.

Most of the instruments you record will produce a lot of noise as well as music, particularly distorted electric guitars. The cure for this type of unwanted sonic phenomenon is the noise gate. Sometimes it's best to leave gating until the mix, sometimes it's better done during track laying. For instruments that aren't usually played with a particularly high degree of subtlety, such as the aforementioned distorted electric guitar, it's fine to do the gating as you record the instrument, and then you have the gate free for something else during the mix. But whatever else you gate, it's almost never a good idea to gate the vocals. Vocalists are so unpredictable, and their contribution to the song so important, that you can't risk losing any sound they make by using a slightly over-eager gate in the signal path. It's hard to gate out things like breaths anyway and I've taken to copying the finished vocal to a spare track, for safety, and carefully spot erasing any noises I don't want to hear in the mix.

Of course, what you do depends on the type of sound you are aiming at, sometimes a thick arrangement will cover odd little noises on the multitrack and sometimes they may even add to the overall texture. When recording sequenced synths and samplers it's easy to get carried away with the idea that since they are pretty well a controlled sound source in the first place you can just 'bung them down' onto tape, but with some synths, the small amount of noise they make quickly builds up if you lay several tracks with the same instrument.

Another source of annoyance at the mixdown stage is when instruments or vocals vary in level a lot. This means that it's hard to get a good balance without dodging the fader up and down simply to compensate for this defect rather than to enhance the mix. The tool for dealing with this is the compressor, either at the recording stage or at the mix. Compression during recording is theoretically better because it doesn't boost tape noise, but for important tracks like vocals I prefer to record clean and then use processing later.

Apart from the inevitable unpredictable problems that always seem to crop up, the big problem with multitrack masters is that they will in all probability have more music recorded on them than will be used in the mix. Perhaps there will be two or three tracks containing attempts at the guitar part, all of which sound good but you don't know which to use. Unfortunately, you will only know when you hear them in context with the tracks all properly treated and balanced. Obviously, it's no problem if there is an entire track that can be dispensed with, but usually you want to keep part of one track, part of another etc etc. It's all part of the job.

Strategies

There is no one right way to go about mixing a multitrack tape. But there are a number of techniques you can employ that will get you up and running with the mix, or which may come to your rescue if things don't seem to be getting anywhere. My favourite way of working, perhaps because it suits the style of my music, is to concentrate on getting the best out of each track in turn, and then go about putting them together in a defined order following a master plan. Let me elaborate...

Individual tracks on the multitrack usually fall into two categories: thin and weedy needing extra support, and over thick and congested needing 'sharpening up'. The third category of tracks that are in-between and therefore just right is so small that it can be neglected for all practical purposes! Actually, you can look positively on problems as a necessary part of the creative process because in solving these problems you'll give your music an individual style that simply wouldn't come about if everything went smoothly. As with everything in life, you have to take the rough with the smooth, but a bit of rough can sometimes make things much more interesting!

The first category of 'thin' sounds usually covers clean samples from a drum machine or sampler and unprocessed synth sounds. In the early days of drum machines, sequencers and DX type synthesisers this thinness was a problem because processing equipment was still very expensive and multi-effects units unheard of. Now we have a whole range of tools at our disposal and there is no excuse for a thin, weak mix that gets sand kicked in its face every time it goes down to the beach. But let's examine some of the thickening tools and potions we have at our disposal, but remember to leave a little cornflour in the kitchen for the Sunday dinner gravy.

Thickening of weak sounds can be done at any stage from track laying to mixdown. One of the best thickeners is to play the sound through an amplifier and speaker and mic it up. This is good not only for guitars but for synths and samplers too, and even vocals if you're after an interesting effect. Even in these days of super-electronic, hyper-computerised mega-effects, a small guitar practice amp, preferably with a few valves in it, can work wonders with a dull lifeless sound. For normal use small amps aren't much good for bass because of the size of the speaker, but for recording this doesn't matter because if you put the mic near the cone you'll find all the bass you need, and the miked up sound can always be mixed with the clean, dry, sound if necessary. If you're doing this in the mix, the only problem is that the sound from the amp will prevent proper monitoring, unless you can put it in a separate room. If you have a spare track, then simply copy the beefed up sound to that, then mix as normal.

One thickener that can be over-used is reverb. You get a nice thick sound all right but sometimes the music gets drowned in a swimming pool acoustic. When using reverb as a thickener, there are two options which you can blend to taste. The first is to use a very short reverb at a fairly high level. A gated reverb is even better because you get the bulk of the effect very close in time to the original sound. It doesn't sound so much as though it has had artificial reverberation added, but it does have more body.

The other thing to do is to add reverb to a track in mono. Is this hard to credit in such a stereo conscious age? But yes it does actually work and it's very often preferable to stereo reverb because the mono version 'sticks' to the sound where stereo reverb separates out into the left and right speakers. If you haven't tried it, then have a go right now, but remember to pan the reverb to exactly the same direction as the signal. With stereo reverb, usually everything is sent to the same reverb unit via a single auxiliary send on the console, but the best way to do mono reverb is to patch it into the channel insert point, if your reverb unit has a reverb balance control that is.

Still on thickening but bypassing compression, chorusing and flanging because they are well known as thickeners, the console's EQ can also be used to beef up sounds. Many new engineers start EQing by boosting whatever frequencies they feel they need more of. But sometimes the EQ can be used to cut frequencies as well. Every instrument has a certain frequency range in which it is most powerful. If you boost this range, you make the instrument almost into a caricature of itself, just as a cartoonist will exaggerate a politician's most prominent feature. But if you cut this frequency range, then you will let the other frequencies the instrument produces come through as well. Once again the only way is to try it, but it certainly works and can be a powerful technique.

When you are recording live instruments the problem is more likely to be that the instruments are not clear enough. In this case, EQ boost as described above can be applied. In extreme cases, a graphic equaliser can be used to filter out the rubbish surrounding the signal you want, but apart from this there are fewer options to make a sound more clear than there are to muddy it up a little.

The skyscraper

Once I have all the individual sounds as I want them, without processing them to extremes, I start to build up the mix. I'm not using 'build' in a loose sense, but as in the erection of a skyscraper I mean lay the foundations, construct the frame work, top it out, and then attach the cladding. A pretty good analogy, even if I did think of it myself.

The foundations of the mix will probably be the drums and bass line, although this may not necessarily be the case. But with a rhythmic piece it's most important to get the rhythm section to support the rest of the structure properly. I would start by setting the bass drum so that the meters read about 10dB under maximum recording level, as a rule of thumb, and then balance the snare according to the type of drum pattern. After this, I bring in the bass line and the rest of the drums in whatever order I feel like, but I spend time making sure that they all pull together in the same direction. If I get it right at this stage the rest will be easy.

The framework consists of the 'pad' instruments – those which are there to fill in the harmonic structure. If the pad is synth strings from my near-antique Roland Alpha Juno 2, then I pan the outputs left and right and bring the channels up to a level where they fit snugly against the bass line – not too quiet, but not competing for attention with the bass. At this stage I can top the structure out by bringing up the vocal line, or melody synth line if it's an instrumental piece which most of mine are. The rest of the mix is simply cladding, it's there to fill in the gaps and keep the chill wind of boredom getting in. A bit of decoration doesn't go amiss either, at the right level.

Following this structural plan is very straightforward if all your sounds are good, or you have made them good. Hopefully once you start bringing up the faders you will only need an odd tweak at the

EQ to bring everything together. Reverb will also be necessary, mainly to fill in any structural gaps which are left.

The map

Figure 13.1 shows another route towards a good mix. Instead of building a skyscraper, you draw a map. Imagine that the speakers are a window into another world, a world of sound if you like, and you are drawing a plan view of that world and all the sounds have their own positions on that map. The first thing to do is to work out from the track sheet where you would like all the instruments to go. Important instruments will obviously come nearer the front, supporting instruments will be further back. Once you have a plan, with specified instruments rather than my more generalised diagram, you can start putting it into action. The easiest part is positioning the instruments between the left and right speakers with the pan control, but also you have to move them forwards and backwards. To send an instrument to a more remote point in the audio landscape you have to do three things: lower the level; cut high and low frequencies; add reverb. These three things are very easy to do, but it's not so easy to do them in the right balance so that it really seems that the instrument is further away, but listen very carefully to what you are doing to each instrument as you move it, and consider whether it actually has moved to where you want it to be.

Whereas a mix done well according to the skyscraper method will have the principal characteristics of clarity and punchiness, a mix done by the map method will sound 'natural', 'organic', 'orchestral'. It's not

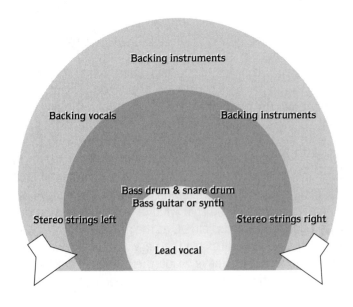

Fig 13.1 The 'map' method of mixing

easy to choose adjectives to describe music, but I hope you have the flavour of what it's all about.

Random factors

Harnessing the random element in music can be a great aid to creativity. One way to do this in mixing is to throw the faders up on all tracks to random levels and then have a good hard listen to what you have got. If these random levels turn out to give a good mix then you will indeed have been extraordinarily lucky, but on the other hand if there is no value whatever in the chance relationships between the various instruments, then that in its turn is very bad luck. The idea is to listen carefully to what you have got, and then make adjustments to turn a chance mix, with some good points, into a wholly good mix with some features that you wouldn't have put in yourself if you had worked all day at it.

Sometimes, when you have had a hard day at the console and things seem to be getting nowhere, the only answer is to turn to lady luck and see what she has to offer – but this isn't an act of desperation, it's another creative tool and fortunately for us it costs nothing and is tax free.

Spock: "Random factors seem to have operated in our favour, Captain."

Kirk: "You mean we've been lucky?"

The elusive perfect mix

There may be no such thing as the perfect mix, but there is such a thing as the best mix you can possibly do within the capabilities of your equipment and surroundings. If you don't emerge from your mixing session feeling totally mentally exhausted then there must lurk at the back of your mind the possibility that you could have done better, this is what distinguishes the real recording engineering men and women from the boys and girls. But even if it's hard work, it's a lot of fun too, and the feeling of achievement you get when things go better than you possibly could have hoped makes it all worth while.

Here, I would like to present a multi-course meal of food for thought, ranging from how an engineer listens to the sound he produces right through to how to present your tapes so that the next engineer down the line towards the cassette or CD knows that he is dealing with the work of a professional. Here goes...

Setting levels

This is the principal function of mixing, to set all the fader levels to achieve a well balanced result. Obviously, what you consider to be a well balanced mix is purely a matter of taste, but there are some points to watch out for, and some tricks to make life easier.

The first thing to do is to listen carefully to the roughly balanced track and find a section which you think can be mixed without moving the faders as the track plays through. The longer this section is the better, although it must always include the most important part of the music – the melody, chorus or hook. If your multitrack can cycle automatically over this section then it's worth spending a few seconds to set the loop points. With the machinery running the section over and over you can experiment all you like to get the right balance. When you get to a stage where you think you are almost there, consider each instrument individually and, without moving the fader, try to decide whether it would be an improvement if you increased or cut its level.

With the vocal, it's very important to remember that by now you know the song very well indeed and have already probably heard it more times than any listener will want to in the future. It's an easy trap to fall into to balance the vocal too low simply because you are 'hearing' it clearly in your mind's ear. It has to be clear even to a first time listener, unless of course it's one of the aims of the production to make the listener struggle a little, which is sometimes no bad thing.

When you have mixed this one most important section, mark the faders with a chinagraph pencil so there is no risk of losing the levels you have set with an inadvertent brush of the elbow. When you play the rest of the track it is almost inevitable that what works for one section doesn't work for another. The only way to do it is to go over and over each section working out what the best levels should be, bearing in mind that you are going to have to move the faders at the right times while the mix is rolling. With my own work, I often find that I have, as well as faders which stay put, as many as ten faders with two or more chinagraph marks reminding me of the level changes I have decided upon. By the time you have worked all this out, you'll know when to make the movements.

Sometimes it's not the best thing to do to set a level by moving a fader, sometimes a slight adjustment of the EQ can achieve a better result because you are adding level at a frequency at which it is needed, and not boosting non-essential frequencies unnecessarily.

Managing noise

Argh! Noise again. Even in the dbx'ed, dolbied and digitalised 1990s we still have to battle against noise almost constantly. A multitrack recording made with dbx, Dolby C, Dolby S and even a digital multitrack will still suffer from noise. For one thing, every track you put down adds a little extra noise which the recorder can do nothing about. But more than that, what happens when you mix separately recorded tracks together is that every time you double the number of tracks in use you get in theory 3dB extra noise. In practice the amount of added noise might be more or less than this figure according to the levels at which you use the tracks, but the fact remains that when you play back a multitrack tape you are bound to hear quite a lot of noise among the music.

The only way to deal with multitrack noise is to fade or cut tracks not in use. This can give a very clean mix with tracks springing up into life out of total silence, if done well. A mix automation system will of course do all this for you, once you input the necessary data. Noise gates on every channel are a great help too, but we don't all necessarily aspire to these heights of grandeur (and expense!). MIDI controlled muting, as mentioned in Chapter 14, is also a brilliant noise killer.

With fewer facilities, there is still quite a lot you can do to reduce noise when mixing from multitrack. The most basic, and least automated, way is to fade tracks manually. Noise is usually most audible at the beginning and end of the track, when very often not all the instruments are in use. All you have to do is fade in noisy instruments just before they come in at the beginning, and out just after they finish at the end. Sometimes it's possible to subgroup a number of tracks so you can do it more easily on fewer faders.

A simple automated noise reducing technique uses just one stereo noise gate with the channels linked (Figure 13.2) so they both open

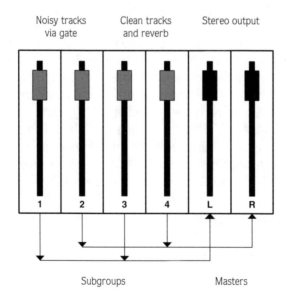

Fig 13.2 Gating the tape tracks cuts the noise when the music finishes and allows the reverb to decay into absolute silence

and close at the same time. If the mix comes to a definite end rather than fades, then you will probably hear noise when the instruments finish but before the reverb dies away completely. In this case simply sub group all the instrumental tracks and put them through the gate before adding the reverb to them in the mix. This way, when the tape tracks finish they will be cut, allowing the reverb to continue and decay into silence. One problem that can crop up with this is that at the beginning of the track, the gate can 'soften' the initial attack. This is solved by starting the mix with the noise gate active but set to zero attenuation when closed, so that in effect there is no gating at all. But immediately after the music starts, turn the control to full gating so that when the track ends it cuts the noise as described.

Using delay

Once upon a time, delay was the effect to use. Would we remember Elvis now without it? Well probably we would, but even if we don't use delay in quite the same way now, it's a very good technique for enlivening a mix that would otherwise fall a bit flat. A delay unit can produce either a single repeat or, by feeding some of the output back to the input, a continuing echo. Which you use must be determined by the needs of the track.

Usually, it's best if the delay time is related to the tempo of the track. This wasn't too easy in the days of tape delay, but with the digital variety available in our multi-effects units there's no problem adjusting the delay in millisecond increments until it sounds right, or taking the short cut and calculating it. The simple way to calculate delay times is to divide the tempo in beats per minute (which you can probably read from the sequencer you used, otherwise you'll have to use a stopwatch and count) into 60,000. This gives the delay time for one beat or quarter note in milliseconds. For instance, if the tempo is 120 BPM, then the delay time is 500ms. If you don't want to use a quarter note (crotchet) delay, then you can get an eighth note (quaver) delay by halving this time. To make the delay more interesting you can divide the quarter note delay time by 3 to give an eighth note triplet pattern, or by 1.5 to give quarter note triplets. If you want to be more adventurous, try multiplying the quarter note delay time by 0.2, 0.4 or 0.6 to give quintuplet patterns. With two delays, even more interesting permutations are possible. How about repeats which come two and three eighth notes after the original sound? Try it!

Extra tracks

This isn't strictly a mixing technique but since it's mix related, now seems as good a time as any to mention it. It isn't as widely known as it could be that it's quite possible to extend the capabilities of a 16 track tape recorder to 17, 18 – perhaps even 20 tracks. And no, it doesn't involve synchronising a drum machine or sequencer.

In the old days when few studios had more than eight tracks, engineers had to use this technique all the time, but since we have got used to having more tracks to play with it has been a tendency to think purely of one instrument per track. But in most arrangements, not all the instruments are active at the same time. Let's imagine a song which has a number of saxophone breaks and a guitar solo, but the sax doesn't play during the guitar solo and the guitarist only has that one spot in the song. If you're running short of tracks then the obvious answer is to 'double bunk' them on one track since they are not getting in each other's way. The only drawback is that the mixer settings you make – EQ and fader etc – to suit the sax will probably not suit the guitar when it comes up.

Even when two or more instruments timeshare a single track it is still possible to treat each one differently on the mixer providing you have enough spare channels. If your patchbay has sockets wired

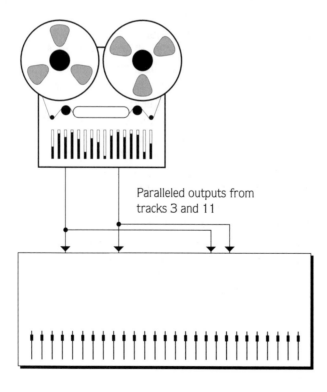

Paralleled outputs from
tracks 3 and 11

Fig 13.3 Provided they don't overlap, two instruments can be recorded on the same track and then connected via parallel outputs to two channels on the console

together in parallel – as it should – you can use these parallels to direct the timeshared track to as many channels as you need on the mixer (see Figure 13.3). The only snag is that you have to mute the sax channel while the guitar is playing and vice versa, but this is still a lot easier than trying to alter EQ, aux and fader settings in a fraction of a second as the mix is running. If you have a MIDI muting system as several modern mixing consoles have, then you can get as many tracks out of your multitrack recorder as you have channels, with the all muting done automatically, with the only restriction being the timesharing involved.

Mixing for others

Mixing your own tracks for the benefit of your own ears is a luxury that the jobbing recording engineer doesn't have. He has to use his own initiative to balance the sounds well and add appropriate effects, but the final guidance will come from elsewhere. As I have said earlier, taking all recording studios from eight track upwards into account, the majority situation is that the engineer is also the producer of the recording. Even if a band is being recorded and one member of the band has styled himself as the 'producer', it is unlikely that his experience in achieving a good recording and mix is as great as the engineer's.

The problem when other people want their say in the mixing process is that they may in all truth not have a clue what they are rabbiting on about. I don't want to appear to be insulting to musicians and budding producers and don't deny their ability to learn how to make excellent recordings given the chance, but from my experience there are a lot of 'experts' on recording who think they know more than they actually do and if the engineer follows what they say to the letter, then the result will be a bad mix. This is where the twin qualities of tact and diplomacy come into play, you can't be a professional recording engineer without them. The ultimate aim is for the band or producer to think that all the creative input into the recording came from them alone, and that the recording engineer was very quick and efficient at following their instructions. In reality, although the mix will hopefully fulfil the producer's requirements absolutely, the recording engineer is usually the driving force behind the creative effort.

The recording engineer's nightmare scenario is where the members of the band who are paying him for the session are all gathered around during the mix throwing comments at him. Usually the vocalist thinks the vocals could be louder, the bass guitarist thinks the mix needs more of him, and so on. It's a funny thing, but no-one ever asks for anything to be quieter. I wonder why?

I was once asked to mix a tape of a five piece band and agreed on the condition that only one band member was present. I was slightly perturbed when all five plus the manager turned up at the studio but only one of them spoke to me during the whole mixing session and they kept their band conferences to the breaks. As a way of working with bands I'd recommend it.

Integration

Particularly with synthesiser music, one of the problems can be getting the whole thing to stick together like it's one piece of music. It's too easy to end up with a lot of instruments playing at the same time, but they don't really sound as though they are playing together. What we need is a way to bring the instruments together as an integral unit. One way to do this is to add a common characteristic to each of the diverse instrumental sounds. It doesn't take too long to think of reverb as the way to achieve this. A little bit of the same type of reverb added to all or nearly all of the tracks, including those tracks which you might have thought didn't need any, can work wonders in bringing everything together. Of course, it's very easy to overuse reverb. You can make the track sound as though all the instruments are playing in the same cathedral, but that's probably not what a recording engineer with any degree of taste would be after, except for a special effect perhaps.

I explained the use of EQ earlier fairly fully in Chapter 11, but I haven't mentioned this application yet. A technique which I am told that painters (artistic painters, not house painters) use to pull all the elements of their work together is to apply a varnish over the whole finished painting. Obviously this has the side effects of making the surface shiny and protecting the painting, but the principal function, apparently, is to integrate the different colours and textures of the paint. The sound equivalent of this can be achieved by passing the entire stereo mix through a graphic equaliser. You may want to use the EQ to add extra depth or brightness, but a few tweaks in the midrange will also help to bring the sounds together by giving them all the same final EQ characteristic.

Thoughts on monitoring

Monitor speakers, and their environment, have two distinct and not necessarily compatible requirements. In no particular order of importance these requirements are 1) to enhance the sounds produced by the musicians and act as an aid to musical creativity; 2) to tell the engineer what's going down onto tape. As you can see, they are both essential but almost entirely they are mutually exclusive.

For decades, top recording studios went for the biggest and loudest monitors they could afford. Some speakers were more accurate than others, but sheer weight of sound lends excitement in itself, so all concerned could get all the 'vibe' (I think that's one of the words they used back then) they wanted from the music, and the sound could still be a reasonably accurate representation of what was on the tape. There's a trend towards smaller speakers these days, and if I may be permitted to say it I think there's no such thing as a good small loudspeaker. There are some small speakers that are good considering, and I'm not denying that small speakers have their uses in the correct situation, but the laws of physics give all the advantages to big 'uns.

KRK Exposé studio monitors

Small speakers – or near field monitors as they have come to be known – were originally used to assess how a mix would sound on a transistor radio or domestic radiogram. As the quality of stereo systems has increased so has the quality of the near field monitors, and used for their intended function they give the engineer a good deal of useful information.

The principal problem is that small speakers lack bass. Sometimes they do sound quite bassy, but if you compare them side by side with a larger speaker you'll realise how much is missing. The temptation is that if you don't hear much bass coming out of the speakers, then you'll add more to the mix to compensate. If you do this, then when someone does come to play the mix on larger speakers, it will sound much more bassy than you intended, and believe it or not there can be such a thing as too much bass! Adding bass to excess also causes headroom problems where the speaker runs out of excursion because of the deep bass, and mid band loudness suffers as a result. The moral is to think twice before adding bass when you're monitoring on small speakers.

My feeling is that since there's no such thing as the perfect speaker, the best way to get a good mix is to listen to your recordings on as many systems as you can, including the car stereo, to get a feel of how well or how badly they travel. Remember that, unless you're playing back on a really dodgy system, if the mix sounds bad then it's the engineering that's at fault. A mix which only sounds good in the studio is by no means a good mix.

Golden ears

Ears are funny things. They don't just look funny on the side of your head but they can sometimes hear things which aren't really happening. I was once mixing a band and the guitarist asked for a little more brightness on the lead guitar. I thought that, if anything, the guitar was already too bright, but since he was the one with the cash I thought I had better appease him, but add as little extra top as possible because I really thought it would spoil the mix and he would regret it later. I reached for the high frequency EQ control and turned it clockwise an infinitesimal amount. "Is that OK?", I asked hopefully. "A bit more", he replied. I gradually edged it up more and more and the guitar was getting brighter and brighter, but still he wanted more top end. Eventually I reached a point where it was so bright it hurt, and the guitarist decided it was just about OK.

I never told him, because he was satisfied with the end result, that although both of us had heard the guitar getting brighter because of the extra high frequency EQ I was applying, we had both been fooled.

I had accidentally grabbed the HF control of a channel I wasn't using and I was turning that. I wasn't changing the guitar sound at all, but because we both thought it was happening, we heard it. As I said, ears are funny things, and easily fooled.

More mixing techniques

14

I wouldn't like to pretend that I know everything there is to know about mixing. Far from it, in fact I don't suppose anyone knows everything that can possibly be known about mixing 4, 8, 16, or 24 or more tracks into stereo. If you look on the bright side, then this means that there is much to be discovered in the way of new tricks, techniques and methods of operation. And with so many people having home studios it stands to reason, and the law of averages, that new developments will come increasingly from people currently outside the inner circle of major professional studios. In this chapter I'm continuing with the theme of explaining established procedures and ways of doing things. Combine these with techniques of your own invention and we'll go a long way towards achieving an ideal combination of creativity and professionalism.

Automation

More years ago than I care to remember when I was studying for some very important exams I found an excellent way of relieving the tension and nerves. I took three tennis balls that happened to be lying around among the debris in my bedsit and taught myself how to juggle. I practised first with one ball to get the feel of throwing it up so that it would land in my other hand without consciously having to catch it. Then I added another ball and practised swapping the two back and forth. The third ball was a little more tricky because you have to keep them all moving and there is always one ball in mid air. My efforts at juggling tennis balls were rather better than my exam grades, but I never did manage to add that elusive fourth ball.

Mixing a multitrack tape into stereo requires many of the skills of a juggler, but there can be as many as sixteen, twenty-four or even up to forty-eight balls in the air at the same time. And what's more, there can be people gathered around you shouting 'useful' advice at you such as, 'Can you get that one a little higher', 'I think you should drop it a bit there', and suchlike. I have a lot of admiration for any engineer who can do a 'live' mix without the help of an automation system and remember perhaps ten, twenty, or more level changes during the song and perform them all in the right place with faultless accuracy, but this is part of the job and with enough practice it can become almost second nature.

The biggest problem of juggling levels during the mix is that you can't sit back comfortably and listen to what's going on. So even if you can do all the level changes with a reasonable degree of ease, you are not able to put all your concentration into the music, where it should be. Automation systems which can remember all the fader movements of the mix may have a 'de-skilling' effect on the actual physical process of mixing, but the engineer now has more time to think about the sounds he is creating.

Most automation systems are still very expensive. The top systems such as those found on SSL and Neve consoles aim to give a sound quality and degree of control as high as that obtainable in a manual mix. Lower cost systems, which are still very pricey add-ons to a console, use lower quality VCAs (voltage controlled amplifiers) which compromise sound quality slightly, and provide a finite number of fader positions so that particularly when the fader is at a low setting, you can hear the stepwise level changes as you fade up or down slowly. But despite these slight drawbacks, the musical benefits you gain can be enormous. I look forward to a day when automation is truly affordable and widespread in the way that mixing consoles have become in recent years.

Yamaha 02R automated digital mixing system

Mixing in sections

One way to get many of the benefits of automation without the expense is to mix in sections. The only equipment you need to be able to do this is a reel-to-reel tape recorder, and a tape editing kit will come in handy too. Songs usually fall into verse and chorus sections, probably with an introduction and middle eight also. If you're unlucky, then you'll find that at the changes between the sections there are too many fader movements to be done manually. In this case, it's possible to mix the verses and get them right and record them to stereo tape, and then go back and mix the choruses and so on. When all the sections have been mixed, it's a simple matter of cutting them back together into a continuous piece of music. Sounds too simple? Well it's not all that easy to get right. The song has to be suitable for mixing in sections for a start, with easily identifiable edit points.

The way you mix the song is important too. It is virtually essential to have a solid foundation that stays the same throughout the song. Then, if it's only the superstructure that needs adjusting, you won't get any significant level changes at the joins, at least you won't on your second or third try. Mixing in sections is a technique that's well worth having a go at and getting the hang of. Once you have it in your repertoire, then you'll be able to recognise the situations where it's going to be of benefit.

Spin in

When no-one but the very fewest of the few had samplers, a casual phrase like 'I locked it into the AMS and spun in it', turned the rest of us a medium shade of green with envy because we still had to do it the hard way. Doing it the 'hard way' is sometimes still a valuable option because, let's face it, we don't all have access to the latest in stereo samplers with a fortnight's worth of memory at 48kHz. Fortunately this advanced sounding technique can be achieved with as little high-tech equipment as a humble cassette deck. It may take a bit longer but the result can be almost as good.

'But exactly what is a spin in?', comes a question from the back. One problem that all recording sessions have is getting all the choruses in the song to sound equally good. And since it's very often the chorus that provides the hook that makes people buy the record, every repeat has to be absolutely perfect. Fortunately, since choruses have the basic feature of repetition, if we find that it isn't possible to get them all as good as they should, if one does happen to be right, then we can use that throughout the song. One way to do this would be to mix the song and make several copies of the chorus and do a cut and past job. This doesn't really work because if the chorus is exactly the same each time, then it will become boring. So what we need to do is to repeat the problem elements – usually the lead or backing vocals.

The term 'spin in' comes from the old procedure that was used in years B.S. – before sampling. That was to mix the backing vocals, or whatever, onto a stereo tape, edit the tape so that it would start and end nice and neatly, and then record it back onto the multitrack. You don't need to have synchronisation to do this since it's possible to get it right in just a few tries, and it's easy to make marks on the tape to cue you in. With a cassette deck as the spin in source (I know that not everyone uses DAT or reel-to-reel) it takes a little longer and a few more tries, but this is what recording is all about really – take that extra bit of time and make it perfect. Once you have the knack of this little trick, then you can laugh at those people who bought expensive samplers to do it, because it's costing you absolutely nothing.

MIDI muting

Automation is expensive, but you can get much of the power of automation with a MIDI muting system. Some consoles offer this as standard, some as an extra. MIDI muting systems need to work in conjunction with a sequencer synchronised to the multitrack tape.

A combination of mutes can be set up which becomes a program, and different programs can be selected via MIDI Program Change messages. Sometimes it's possible to use Note-on and Note-off messages, but the end result is the same. A mix always sounds so much cleaner if none-contributing tracks are switched off, and this is very difficult to do manually. MIDI muting systems should be made compulsory equipment on every console, in my opinion.

DAT mastering

Mastering onto DAT has a lot of advantages compared to reel-to-reel tape. For one thing it's extremely cheap in comparison, and that means that you can afford to take a few more chances with the mix and use a lot more tape. (In the heyday of reel-to-reel mastering, the amount of tape that went into the bin was nothing short of amazing. DAT is definitely the medium of choice for the Green engineer, and also for budget conscious studios since the initial capital cost and run-

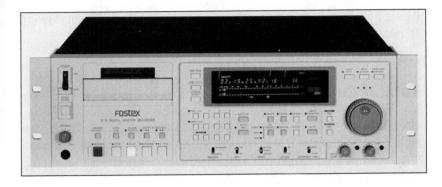

ning costs of DAT are a lot less than the quarter-inch alternative. The only disadvantage of DAT is that if you want to edit your recording, then you are going to have to shell out the readies. The cost of an editing suite per hour or day is pretty high compared to that of a razor blade and splicing tape.

When mastering onto tape (reel-to-reel), the procedure is to record first and then edit the chosen mixes together with leaders and spacers to make up a continuous running programme, perhaps part of an album. There is a strong temptation to try to do the same with DAT and assemble a DAT tape of completed mixes. I would recommend however that you don't do this and leave any assembly until the copying stage when you'll have to hire or borrow a second machine. It's hard enough to mix a track well without having to worry about getting it onto the tape in the right place as well.

The best way to mix onto DAT is to use one DAT tape per track. Yes it costs more, but remember the savings you have already made. If you do it this way there is absolutely no risk of erasing another track on the same tape and wasting perhaps a day's work or more. I would go further than this and say that if the mix is an easy one with few fader movements, then you do an identical mix onto another tape for safety.

Chances are that you'll have several attempts at the mix and since you have plenty of room on the tape you can have several attempts and choose the best later, recording over only the ones where you made obvious mistakes. Once you have the definitive mix, it's also worthwhile making another pass with the vocal 3dB higher. If there is a risk of mixing anything too low, when judged in the clear light of the next day, then it's bound to be the all-important vocal. Doing the 'extra voice' mix saves you having to start again from scratch.

When you are sure that you have the ideal mix among several attempts on the DAT tape, remember to label the inlay card with the Start ID number of the one you want. When you come to the copying stage, if you're anything like me then you'll have forgotten which one it was meant to be and have to sit down to a lengthy listening session to decide which take was the best.

Total recall

Unless you're one of those insufferable people who always gets it right first time, then it's often the case that when you mix a track it sounds really great when you've finished – but next morning it sounds terrible. One reason for this is 'ear fatigue', which has both physical and psychological causes. Another reason is that you really need to be able to stand back and get a perspective view before you can mix properly, this is one of the reasons re-mixers have had such a success. People who do this have the luxury of being able to listen to a multi-track tape and jettison a line that took several hours and buckets of blood, sweat and tears to record. Could you do the same?

The chances are that your first mix of a song will be great, apart from one tiny but important detail – like the vocal being inaudible perhaps. But once you have zeroed the console and lost the settings it may be impossible to get back to what you had before and correct the mistake, unless you have an expensive mixing console that has

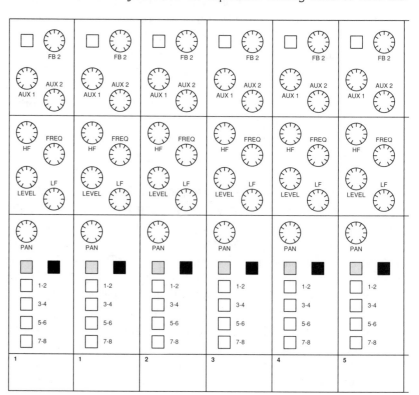

Fig 14.1 Part of a plot sheet for a mixer

recall facilities. A technique used by theatre sound engineers to recall settings from performance to performance is the plot sheet (Figure 14.1). This is a diagram showing all the controls on the mixer on which you superimpose the settings you use and note any effects. I've included part of a plot sheet for the mixer in my home studio that I made up using desk top publishing software on my computer. When I've completed a particularly difficult mix, I spend time filling in this sheet, and I have to report that when I've done it, I've never regretted it. When I've been lazy and not filled it in – that's when I wish I had. It's certainly not as quick as a computerised recall system, but it works and it's a lot less expensive.

Tape presentation

Let's assume that you have been hard at work, recording an album's worth of songs, and you have the finished stereo master recordings spread over a number of DAT cassettes. In the days of reel-to-reel you would edit up a finished master reel, in sequence as it would appear on the end product, in your studio. With DAT this is possible but impractical. You may if you wish produce a compilation tape, by digitally copying from one DAT machine to another, but you won't be able to get the gaps between items as short as you probably want them. You will also probably have slightly untidy starts to each track with a second or so of tape hiss from the multitrack. Also, horror of horrors, the levels may be different from track to track. What you need is a trip to a CD mastering studio to sort things out professionally.

Turning a collection of DAT tracks into a CD is a process of copying them, in the correct manner and under your supervision, onto a Sony 1630 cassette. This will be sent, by a trusted carrier, to the CD factory where it will be used to make the glass master from which all the copies will be produced. The CD factory isn't in the business of making artistic decisions and whatever is on the 1630 tape will be on the CD.

The first thing you need to know is how to produce a DAT tape that will please the mastering engineer. Bear in mind, if you aspire to professionalism, that the tape is the end product of the studio process, on which the standard of your work will be judged. If you have been working on your own project then you may be able to hold the hand of the master tape personally, but in other circumstances you will have to send the tape out into the big wide world and hope it can fend for itself. This means that you won't be around to answer any queries the mastering engineer might have.

Mostly, making a master recording on DAT is an artistic process. It's a very transparent medium and there are few restrictions on what you can put on it. Not like analogue tape where you had to think about whether you were squashing your high frequencies and whether noise was getting to be a problem. With DAT you just set your recording levels as high as you can and get on with it. But you do have to remember two things. The first is to leave the first thirty seconds or so of the tape blank. Actually this should preferably be recorded at zero level, rather than remaining as virgin tape. DAT tapes sometimes get chewed up, and this usually happens when the cassette enters and departs from the mechanism, so if you always rewind the tape before taking it out then any damage will be to the blank section. The second thing to remember is that each track must start with at least 15 seconds of silence leading directly into the music. To make a digital to digital copy, the receiving machine will need to synchronise to the sampling frequency of the signal. The recording must be made continuously, without stopping the tape, from the beginning of the 15 seconds to the end of the track. One last point about the tape itself is that it may be useful to record at the start a 1kHz tone at 10dB below the peak level on your recorder's meters. You can use this as a level reference and state on the DAT inlay card what the peak level of the music is relative to this tone. And by the way, when your DAT tape is finished, don't forget to click open the write-protect tab.

Let's suppose you have compiled your master recordings digitally onto a single DAT tape in the correct sequence for the album, but necessarily with gaps that are too long. You may be attending the CD mastering session yourself or you might have passed the tape on to your client. Either way, the tape should be presented like this:

The cassette itself (write on the label or directly onto the shell)
- Artist
- Title
- Open the write protect tab

The inlay card

- Artist
- Title
- Date
- Studio
- Engineer's name and contact telephone number
- Sampling frequency

- Pre-emphasis on or off
- Tone level and frequency
- Peak level of programme in decibels with respect to tone
- Numbered list of Start IDs, song titles and durations
- Start time of each item (optional)
- Total duration of tape

There is another point which CD mastering engineers will know about, but many people in the sound industry are as yet not totally familiar with DAT and its problems. You would tend to assume that a Start ID means the start of a track, but this may not quite be the case. If you cue a track ready for playback using the Start ID then it might start a fraction of a second – a significant fraction – late. You might consider writing on the inlay card, "Start IDs for guide purposes only", or "Do not cue using Start IDs", or something similar.

If your DAT cassette is presented according to these common sense guidelines then the mastering engineer will know that he is dealing with the work of a fellow professional. The alternative is amateurish product about which a respected mastering engineer commented, "We get three or four DATs in here a day and only one of those will say who the artist is on the shell. Most of the time it will be unlabelled with the record lugs still enabled. Pick one of those up and you know roughly what you're in for". Let's try and make his life a little more pleasant in future, shall we?

15 Location recording

Recording in the studio is lots of fun. It can be as musically and technically challenging as you like – or as challenging as your customers like – but the one thing you are sure of is that barring equipment malfunction or a power cut, you are in control. But one day, someone will ask you whether you can make a recording outside the cozy confines of your personal playroom. The real world of concert halls and auditoria can present difficulties that the studio-bound engineer never has to face. Often, you will come across a problem that you could not possibly have anticipated, and be expected to solve it almost instantly. This is real sound engineering and I love it. There's nothing quite like walking into a rehearsal, planning how to set up the gear and the mics, and then hearing the results which, hopefully, prove that your plans were well laid.

My personal location recording speciality is in classical concert work so I'll spend most of my time discussing this. There is much in common with other kinds of recording such as band gigs, or any kind of location session recording, so the information will also cover these situations to a large extent. But in case you are worrying that you will be deprived of the fun and satisfaction of solving location recording problems yourself by reading about them here first, let me assure you

Most location recording engineers would envy this degree of luxury

that there is never any shortage of possible things to go wrong and spoil your recordings. The first law of location recording states that whatever you least expect will happen. Just remember that if you are being paid to bring back a good quality tape, you have got to come up with the goods – no-one gets paid for excuses.

First contact

The sort of people who want recordings of classical concerts fall into four categories: musicians and composers; musical societies; concert agents and promoters; special interest groups. They are not going to knock on your door to ask you to record them. Neither are they over responsive to advertising of any kind. So how do you get the work? The only real answer is by word of mouth. If you do one job well, then the chances are that you will get recommended to someone else, then hopefully things will snowball.

The first contact will be a phone call saying that the promoter (I shall use 'promoter' as a generic term to cover the four categories I mentioned) has a concert he or she wants recorded and would you be interested in doing it? Before agreeing, it's necessary to find out a few details first. It's not a good idea to bite off more than you can chew and I wouldn't hesitate to turn a job down if I thought I couldn't do it justice at the fee on offer. Not that I'm overly mercenary, but if I need to use an assistant, then I need extra money. It's as simple as that.

The important details you need to know before accepting the job are these: Obviously the date and location of the recording are vital. As well as the time of the concert you also need to know the time of the rehearsal. The nature of the music to be recorded and the intended end-product will decide whether it's a go/no-go situation. It's up to you to judge your own capabilities, but if you are asked to record Mahler's Symphony of a Thousand for CD release on a major label, and you haven't done any classical recording before, then it's probably better to get some practice on smaller jobs first. Remember that a word-of-mouth reputation can work negatively as well as positively.

Once you know what is being asked of you, then you can quote a fee. I work on a daily rate for my services. Most recording studios charge according to the amount and sophistication of the gear they have available, and the quality of their acoustics etc. I regard the engineer – i.e. myself – as being the most important part of the package so I charge for myself and bring along whatever equipment I think is necessary, incorporating any hire fees into my quote.

Recordings fall into two categories: quality recordings where the promoter wants the best you can offer and will pay for it, and 'quickie' recordings where you are expected to do a reasonable job, but the money on offer is limited. I feel that it's important to make this distinction because if you are going to do a good job, then you need to spend more time and effort on it, setting up your equipment before a full rehearsal of the music to be performed. The 'quickie' recording is where you get a ten minute sound check an hour before the performance starts – or no sound check. Inevitably, the recording will not be quite as good as it might have been, but you have to spend less time on it. It's up to you to work out your rates for a full day, and for a quick sound check and recording. Don't use the word 'quickie' when you are talking to the promoter though!

Planning

When you have agreed to do the recording for a certain fee, there are a few more details to sort out. So far you know these facts:

Date
Location
Time of rehearsal/sound check
Time of concert
Number of musicians and instruments

Before you put the phone down you need to find out whether or not the musicians are going to be arranged conventionally on a stage or whether there is anything unusual about their distribution around the hall. Sometimes there can be a subsidiary choir or band placed in a balcony which will require extra miking. You can't find out everything from a brief conversation but if you know the important facts, then you are already halfway towards your microphone set-up.

Also important is the name of your contact at the concert hall. Concerts are often held in churches and your contact may be the verger or the vicar himself. In a theatre, you contact will be the electrician. Elsewhere, you will be dealing with the caretaker.

Reluctant as I am to generalise on caretakers as a profession, there are some people around who are rather less than helpful when it comes to easing your passage through locked doors and turning the mains on. Finally, during this by now lengthy phone call at the promoter's expense, you need to know the titles and duration of the works being performed, so you know what music to expect and that it will fit on your tape.

Equipment

I work on the principle of taking the minimum amount of gear I need to do a good job. With concert recording, there comes a point where you don't get any better results from having more equipment, unless you go the whole way with multiple microphones and a couple of assistants, which of course will push the fee sky high. I started recording concerts years ago in my student days when I took out a whole truck load of borrowed gear with a couple of mates. This would include a mixing console that took two people to carry, two hefty analogue tape recorders, Dolby A noise reduction units, power amp, loudspeakers, and miles of cable on drums. "Why take two tape recorders?", I hear someone asking. The reason is that unless all of the pieces to be performed are under thirty minutes in duration, you have to be able to swap to another recorder instantly, and edit the tape together later. I still have nightmares about a close shave I had attempting to change reels of tape between the movements of a symphony when I had foolishly taken only one tape machine, thinking that the duration of the piece would be the same as on a record I had.

But the main problem with analogue tape is that it's expensive. You need four or five reels for the average concert, which comes to around sixty or seventy-five pounds. Fortunately, DAT has changed all of this. Most concerts last less than two hours which will fit comfortably onto a 120 minute DAT tape costing a very reasonable sum, and almost infinitely reusable if the master isn't required after copying.

The mixing console I use is the same as I have for multitrack work at home. It isn't anything special, but it has enough facilities, is reasonably quiet and is very portable. For microphones I use a pair of AKG C414s which have been favourites of mine for a long time. I also have a couple of AKG 451s with the CK1 cardioid capsule which are nice and clear, but don't quite have the same 'realism' of the large diaphragm, multi-pattern 414. My mic kit is completed with a Shure SM58 and a Beyer MCE5 tie-clip mic. As you can see, this isn't a lot of mics exactly, but it's in proportion with the type of work I do and the combination works effectively.

Sprouting from the mics are cables, which leads me to another question, "How much cable do you need for the average location recording job?". For my kind of recording in the venues I'm likely to work in I find my 200 metre stock of cable, in 10m and 20m lengths, more than adequate. Sometimes a couple of 10m cables may be enough, but I would hate to be caught short miles from base. The type of cable I use is made by a company called Canary – sorry, Canare. I use a quad cable which has four individual conductors twisted tightly together to give good interference rejection, − rejection, that is, of what little interference gets through the braided screen. It's a small point, but cables are best coloured black for this type of work, to be as inconspicuous as possible to the audience.

My mics are mounted on five boom mic stands of the type to be found in the catalogues of various mic manufacturers. I also have four short stands for inconspicuous use at the front of the stage. Sometimes I can get away without mic stands altogether if there is a suitable balcony at the venue − I sling a rope across and suspend a stereo pair of mics. The rope, by the way, is strong nylon from a ships' chandlers. Mountaineering shops sell ropes that are good for falling off crags because of their elasticity, but it's not a good idea for the mics to droop under their own weight!

For monitoring I either take a pair of Sennheiser headphones, or go the whole hog and take my Quad amplifier and B&W speakers. It is of course better to monitor on speakers, although for simple mic set-ups it is possible to balance effectively on cans. But if I'm doing a full day and know that I will have access to a separate 'control room' I definitely prefer to have my B&Ws with me.

Setting up

When you arrive at the venue, the first thing to do before unpacking any equipment is to find your contact. This is not always easy, and when you do find the right person and announce who you are, you'll probably get the response, "I didn't know there was going to be any recording today." Of course it's the promoter's responsibility to make sure that there is permission to make a recording and that all staff have been forewarned, but it doesn't always happen. The answer is to pretend to be a menial employee of the promoter who will sort it all out when he or she arrives. Don't let anyone delay you setting up whatever you do, use whatever ploys you have to to get the job done. Another important point is that some venues charge a recording fee. The promoter should pay this direct to the management, and not put this administrative task onto you.

Despite what I have said, things usually go reasonably smoothly and there will be someone to help you find a location for your equipment and a mains point. If you can, get hold of a key so that you can lock your gear up while you are not there to look after it. I know to my cost that thieves are are about and on the look out for unguarded valuables, even in churches.

The ideal place to set up your control room is in a room close to the main hall, but physically separated (Fig 15.1). If things are really going well for you, there will be a gap under the door to pass your cables through when the door is shut. Often it is only practical to set up in a quiet corner of the main hall, so you will have to monitor on headphones there. This isn't a desirable situation, but it can still work. The spot to look for is preferably somewhere where there won't be any members of the public during the performance, or at least where they won't be wandering about too much. One point – if you are going to be in the main hall, then you might as well pick a spot where you can see what's going on.

Once you have identified your control position and brought in the gear, it's time for a reconnaissance mission. This is where a little thought can pay dividends. If there is a balcony rail then a pair of mics can be slung on a rope. If there is no balcony, then you will have to use mics on stands. This is where you have to get your priorities right. Remember that people have paid to come to the concert and that you are only 'eavesdropping'. The one place you can't put your mic stand is right in front of the conductor, which is obviously just

Fig15.1 A typical recording setup in a separate room from the performance

Power amplifier and speakers

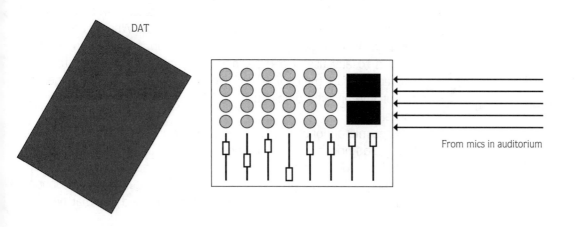

DAT

From mics in auditorium

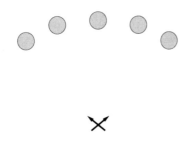

A crossed pair of mics on a small stand is sufficient if the performers are arranged suitably

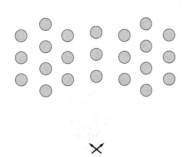

A crossed pair of mics is good for a large choir or ensemble, but it must be positioned fairly high

Preferred mic position

Mics too low to pick up rear of choir

Choir on staging

A low mic position is acceptable for a single row of performers, but it will not pick up the rearmost ranks of a large choir or ensemble

Fig 15.2 Different mic configurations

about the best place for you, but unacceptable to just about everyone else. If there is only one row of performers, mics can be positioned on low stands. A deeper choir or ensemble will need a higher microphone position to capture the sound from those in the rearmost ranks. It isn't always possible to place mics in front of the stage, due to fire regulations. This is something you will only find out about five minutes before the audience is let in, which will completely ruin your plans. Also, you must remember that mics on stage may get in the way of the performers if the stage layout is changed between pieces. I can promise you that unless you can sling your mics, you are going to have plenty of challenges simply finding the right position for them for the sound you want while fitting in with everyone else's problems. Let me give you some examples:

I was asked to record a performance by a Greek choir in a Jewish Synagogue. Not being of that faith, I wasn't prepared for the layout of the performance. There was a raised area where you would find the aisle of a church which was a lot longer than it was broad. I would have liked to sling two pairs of mics to cover it properly, but I only had one rope! Undaunted, I chose my mic position carefully and hoped that the choir would be well balanced internally. All would have been well if the Cantor – the solo singer – had not faced the choir during the performance, which I found out at the last moment. I hadn't asked because I had never come across anything like this before. If I hadn't my multipattern mics with me I wouldn't have had time to set up another mic for the Cantor. Fortunately, I was able to switch the mics to figure-of-eight, which picks up at the rear, and re-angle them slightly. The fact that I came away with a reasonably good recording was down to luck as much as anything else, but I have certainly learned from the experience.

Another 'difficult' experience was in the Purcell Room in London's South Bank arts complex. The promoter had left a message on my answering machine saying that he would like to record a concert the next day. I could only get through to his secretary, who couldn't tell me in much detail what the concert was about. When I turned up, I found a Argentinean guitarist and folk group, none of whom spoke English to any useful degree, and my Spanish is unfortunately non-existent. In fact the only person who could speak both languages was the promoter, who didn't turn up till the very last minute before the concert.

I set microphones in places I thought would be useful, considering that I did know that they were going to play in various combinations, and also a couple at the front of the stage for general pick up. Then a member of the folk group came up to me and said "No microphone" and waved his hands around rather a lot. It turned out that he was a dancer and he needed a clear space to strut his stuff. I put on a determined expression and eventually, after much discussion on his part with the rest of the group, it emerged – as far as I could tell – that he did in fact have enough room to dance, as long as my cables were out of his way, which I made sure they were. The recording was a success.

When the mics are set, the last thing to do is to tape all the cables to the floor with Gaffer tape. This is important because if a member of the public suffers an injury because of your negligence, then you'll find yourself in court. The cables have to be totally taped down, not just at intervals. You could use up to half a reel of two inch Gaffer at some venues, so keep a good stock, and remember to include the cost in your fee.

Rehearsal and performance

The rehearsal is your opportunity to move the mics around for the best result and to check levels. Always ask to hear the loudest part of the music, and allow yourself at least 6dB headroom above that to cope with concert enthusiasm. I like to record part of the rehearsal to check that everything is functioning correctly. Don't play this test recording to anyone if you can help it because they will always find fault, even if the recording is as good as it could possibly be, and you don't want to be put in the position of having to change something you think is right. After the rehearsal there will probably be some time to wait before the concert which you can put to use by going for a bite to eat, if you have secured your equipment. Unfortunately, even if your insurance cover is adequate, it would be immensely inconvenient to lose something so I am always very careful.

When the concert starts you have to be absolutely sure to catch the first beat of the music. With DAT it's not a problem to start the tape early and waste a couple of minutes, to be on the safe side. With old fashioned analogue tape, where you were always pushed for recording duration, it was always a risky business wondering when to start if you couldn't see the performers. On my DAT, I switch off the auto indexing so that I can insert ID markers manually. I mark the start of each piece, and also the very end of the concert after the applause. I'll explain this later. During the concert, things should run smoothly. If you have set your balance and levels correctly there shouldn't be any need to twiddle any knobs, with a simple mic set-up. For each piece it's a good idea to make a note of the highest level reached. This will be useful when it comes to copying later.

At the end of the concert, don't forget that there is almost bound to be an encore or two. In fact, even if you have been told by the promoter, the conductor and anyone else that there isn't going to be an encore – keep that tape running! Even if the blame for missing an encore isn't rightly yours, you'll still get it.

Post production

This usually means making ten or so cassette copies. To make this easy, I look for the ID markers which point out the beginning of each piece, erase and re-record them so that each piece has a nice clean start. At the end of the applause that follows each piece (which is is easily found by backtracking from the next Start ID) I record a Skip ID. This gives me a tape that will play from the beginning of the concert to the end without unnecessary gaps. It's a simple matter to run off a few cassettes while doing the ironing.

The most important part of the proceedings, however, is yet to come – getting paid. I would recommend that until you know your customers, that you see the cash before parting with the master tape or cassettes. Most people are honest of course, but it's best not to take any risks.

The last essential part of the post production process is listening carefully to your recording and thinking about how you can do it better next time. The quest for the perfect recording is never ending and it's unlikely that anyone with high standards will be satisfied. Location classical recording is one of the most enjoyable types of work I do. There's always a new challenge and a new problem to sort out, and if you come away with a good result it makes it all worthwhile.

Equipment list

This is my own checklist for location recording. For special jobs, I would hire in extra equipment.

```
2 x AKG C414
2 X AKG C451/CK1
Beyer MCE5
Shure SM58
6 x mic clips
Stereo bar
4 x small mic stand
5 x boom mic stand
Rope
8 x 10m mic cable
6 x 20m mic cable
2 x jack to male XLR cable
```

4 x jack to phono cable
2 x speaker cable
Mains extension cable
4 way mains adaptor
IEC mains cable
LNE mains cable
Mixing console
Mixer power supply
Mixer power supply cable
Mixer stand
DAT recorder
2 x 120 DAT tape
DAT inlay cards
DAT labels
DAT cleaning tape
Power amplifier
2 x monitor loudspeaker
Headphones
Gaffer tape
Masking tape
Chinagraph pencil
Marker pen
Notebook
Pen
Torch
Toolkit
Venue address
Promoter's name and phone number
Contact's name and phone number
Business cards

find a particular passage of music on a record than it is on tape. This is due to the two dimensional access we now have available.

So with a record, we find it much easier to 'go to bar 556', because of the easy access. The problem remains that bar 556 is not identified on the record as it is on the musical score – unless you count the record grooves as you traverse the disc. If we had a recording system that offered two dimensional access together with proper identification of the different sections of the music then we would have a system that offered as much scope for controlling and editing music as real musicians have – and of course it would play the right notes every time.

Hard disk recording

A comparatively recent arrival in the studio world is the hard disk recording system. It uses techniques developed by the computer industry to provide two dimensional access of digital recordings, with identification of the timing of the programme content and musical sections (although I refer to music, it could just as well be segments of speech). It seems ideal as a storage medium for music, and in many ways it is ideal. But let's look first at exactly what a hard disk is.

Most of us are familiar with floppy disks, used in computers, samplers, sequencers and synthesisers to store data. If you open the casing of a floppy disk (not one you intend to use again!), you will find a flexible plastic disk with a magnetic coating, very similar to the coating on magnetic tape. Indeed, you could consider it to be magnetic tape, but made into a different shape and slightly stiffer.

Inside the disk drive of the computer, or sampler or whatever, there is an arm roughly similar to the pick-up arm of a record player, which is able to traverse the rotating disk, under the direction of the

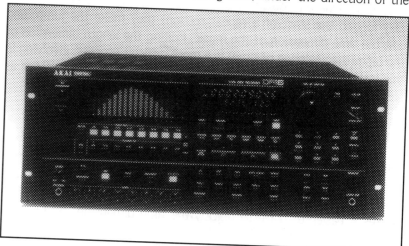

Akai DR16 16-track hard disk recorder

disk controller circuitry and software. On the end of the arm is a magnetic head, similar to the heads of a tape recorder. The disk's magnetic head is optimised for the conditions under which it works, and can play back (read) as well as record (write).

A hard disk is very similar to a floppy disk, but with some important differences: The hard disk drive contains several disks mounted on a common spindle. These disks are rigid and are never removed (except in the case of some cartridge types, which have a fairly small capacity). The unit is sealed to prevent contamination of the disk surfaces.

Figure 16.1 shows the internal structure of a typical hard disk unit. In this instance, there are six active disk surfaces, each with its own read/write head and head positioning arm. The heads do not touch the surface of the disk but ride above it on a lubricating film of air.

The advantage of the hard disk over the floppy disk is that the data can be much more densely packed. Because the disks are rigid and protected from contamination, the heads can be allowed to ride much closer to the disk's surface. Magnetic theory states that the closer the head is to the recorded data the more tightly packed the data can be. Even so, the data storage density is not as high as digital tape. With tape, the heads can get even closer to the recorded data.

Let's assume for the moment that one channel of digital audio is to be recorded onto the hard disk. Figure 16.2 shows the organisation of data storage into blocks, tracks, cylinders and sectors. Each of the circular tracks on each disk surface is divided into a number of blocks. The block is the smallest possible unit of storage and will contain a

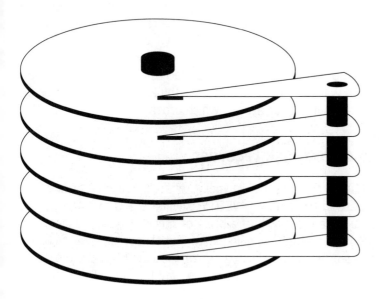

Fig 16.1 Internal structure of hard disk

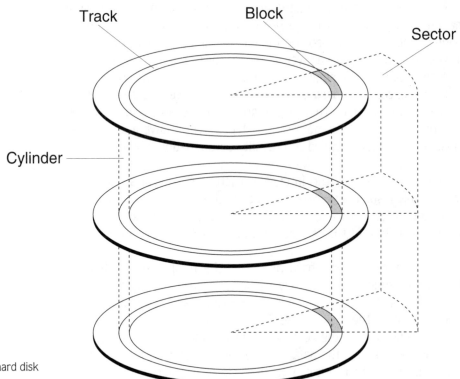

Track Block Sector

Cylinder

Fig 16.2 Data structure of hard disk

number of milliseconds of one channel of digital audio information. (To permit faster storage and retrieval, blocks will probably be grouped together into allocation units). As well as recording the audio data, additional control data is recorded identifying the timing of the audio in the block and its relationship to the rest of the programme. Incoming audio data is split up into blocks which may be recorded at any position on any of the disk surfaces. Continuous music does not have to be recorded in a continuous path across the disk, the controlling software will place the data where it thinks fit, and keep tabs on which blocks should be replayed in which order.

Using the hard disk recorder

Let's now jump to the user's viewpoint of a hard disk recording system – perhaps in front of a 'QWERTY' keyboard and monitor screen. Imagine you have two takes of a piece of music, mixed, finished, and available on a conventional analogue or digital tape storage medium. One take has a wrong note a quarter of the way through, the other has a similar fault three quarters of the way through. The hard disk system is to be used to edit these two takes into a single perfect performance. The first stage of the process is the upload. Starting with the first take, the music is digitally copied onto the hard disk. The two takes will be stored as two sound files, analogous to the text or data files stored on a computer's hard or floppy disk. As Take 1 is copied into File 1, the hard disk recorder will split up the music into blocks of data, and record these blocks separately and probably discontinuously onto the surfaces of the disks. Take 2 is copied into File 2.

Once copied, the hard disk recorder now has virtually instant access to any part of either take. Ask the unit to play Take 1 and Take 1 will start almost instantly. Ask it to play Take 2 and Take 2 will start just a couple of hundred milliseconds after the instruction has been entered. If you want, you can skip about from section to section of the music, in either take, and the hard disk recorder will respond as quickly as you can move the mouse or press the buttons. If you could look inside the hard disk unit, you would see the positioning arms hopping backwards and forwards, extracting the data from the blocks and loading it into a buffer memory from which it would be read out as a continuous stream of data to the digital-to-analogue convertor.

Now, to edit the two takes together, you would find the in and out points in a similar way to ordinary reel-to-reel tape, but controlled by the mouse and keyboard (or whatever alternative controllers the system you are using provides). The essential difference is that with tape you have physically to cut the tape and join it together. Either that or copy the two takes, played on separate machines and switched at the right moment. But with the hard disk recorder, all that is needed is to input the edit decision data. You tell it where to make the join and the hard disk recorder will perform the edit in real time absolutely seamlessly. It doesn't have to copy the result onto a separate area of the disk. All it does is read the data from File 1 up to the edit point, and from File 2 after it. This happens in real time every time you replay the edited version of the music. No data is changed and no copy is made. All this can be done thanks to the speed of access of the hard disk, and software processing of the data. When you are happy with the result, the finished edited performance is downloaded back onto DAT.

Multitrack

So far, all I have discussed is single channel audio recording and of course all that I have said applies to stereo too. What more can hard disk recorders offer? The answer is that they can function as digital multitrack recorders too. Several systems are currently on offer that can provide up to eight-track operation and sixteen-track is possible too. Eight or sixteen tracks may not sound a lot when the high end of the music recording industry runs on pairs of synchronised 24-track machines. But hard disk recorders have other advantages to compensate.

The first point to emphasise is that it doesn't matter to the hard disk itself whether it is being used to record single channel or multiple channel audio. All that is important is that there is enough time for the system to get all the data onto the disk and back off again. A typical hard disk can store perhaps two hours of single channel audio. With the correct number of inputs, outputs, D/A and A/D convertors and the appropriate control software, the same hard disk could record fifteen minutes of eight simultaneous channels. The capacity of a hard disk system is specified in terms of the number of track-minutes it can accommodate. The recorder itself may be capable of handling several hard disk drives – how many you have depends on what you intend to use the system for, and how much you can afford to pay.

As far as editing the eight tracks goes, the procedure is the same as in the single channel example given earlier but another important advantage an eight track hard disk recorder has over eight track tape is that the tracks can be slipped backwards and forwards against each other in time. For music, this means that a lagging synth part, say, can be replayed a few tens of milliseconds earlier to compensate. In film dubbing (one of the major uses of hard disk recorders), layers of sound effects can be easily synced up to the action. To do this with tape means copying onto a separate recorder, adjusting the timecode offset, and re-recording back onto the multitrack – a time consuming procedure.

A second advantage is that although only eight tracks can be replayed at any one time, there could be any number of musical segments contained on the hard disk, up to the limit of its capacity. There could be a dozen takes of a guitar solo, or a vocal, but only the best would be chosen and allocated to an output. More than this, the twelve takes could be edited – using the edit decision concept once again – to combine the best parts of each. Producing an extended mix, or perhaps a two and a half minute radio version, of a song would also be child's play compared to the endless copying and editing required to do the same thing with tape.

System limits

Hard disk recorders do have their limitations. The major limiting factor is the access time necessary to retrieve a piece of audio information from the disk. To move the head to the correct location takes a few milliseconds, and the music can't wait. The time that is lost moving the head is made up by reading the data faster than real time into the buffer memory which can then read it out at the correct speed, but there is a finite limit. With any system the shorter the segments and the more they have been moved around, the more likely it is that segments will be skipped on playback. This also applies when lots of crossfades are used because this is usually done by creating a short new file for each fade. But as with most areas of hardware and software development, things are getting better all the time.

There are also other problems peculiar to hard disk recorders. You may have noticed one already: 'These disks are rigid and are never removed' is a quote from an earlier paragraph. A typical hard disk editing session would start with uploading the disk from tape – a procedure that takes as long as the recording itself – and end with downloading the result back to tape. Time is money, and some hard disk recorder manufacturers rationalise this by saying that you will probably want to listen to the music and make some editing decisions anyway before the session starts properly. And when you have finished, you can audition the result and make a cassette copy during download. If you just wanted to store the products of a session overnight before continuing, then a special tape storage system is sometimes available. This can store the contents of the hard disk on tape cartridges, freeing the disk itself for other use. This kind of tape storage works more quickly than real time, and subsequent upload is faster too.

Optical disk

The newest of the new recording media is the erasable optical disk, sometimes known by its full title of magneto-optical disk. You can think of this as a cross between a hard disk and a compact disc (the spelling of 'disk' and 'disc', by the way, follows standard industry usage).

An optical disk comes in a cartridge and may be inserted into an optical disk drive. Storage capacity of the $5^1/_4$ inch type is around two hours of stereo on each of its two sides. Removable hard disks are also available. The drives are inexpensive but the cartridges cost more than opticals. The advantage of the new medium is of course that the disk can be taken away without having to copy its contents onto a back up device or DAT. The disks however are not as yet even remotely comparable in price with DAT. Whether the optical disk will totally replace hard disks is a good question. Optical disks are slower than hard disks and probably always will be, but eight track record

the best that has been achieved in a commercial unit is six-track simultaneous record and eight track replay – at a price.

It isn't clear in the crystal ball whether the future is going to be hard disk or optical disk, but I could speculate and say that very soon, probably sooner than we think, tape will cease to exist as a medium other than for location recording and for final mastering, and all multitrack music recording and subsequent stereo mixing, and editing will be done on disk. For me this time can't come soon enough!

Any questions? 17

Throughout this book I have had two aims in mind. Firstly, to help home recordists get more fun out of their music and their equipment, and secondly to give budding professional engineers a 'leg up' and hopefully point out a few interesting directions worthy of exploration. Now more than ever it is possible to achieve good results from very basic set-ups, and it is also at last possible for anyone who wants to turn pro to have a real chance of getting a shot at the big time. In my various alter egos as lecturer in sound engineering, composer and producer, freelance classical recording engineer (and also general odd-job person it seems) I am often asked questions on my favourite subject which range from the highly intelligent and perceptive (i.e. the ones to which I don't know the answer), to the more practical ("Could you use fewer microphones and give me a discount?"). So I have put a few of these questions together with one or two I've had cause myself to ask in the past. I hope the answers will shed just a little more light on the vast subject of the art of recording engineering.

Can I achieve professional quality recordings on my home equipment?

In a word – yes! That's called positive thinking, but even being more realistic you don't need all that much gear to produce a recording with commercial value (bearing in mind of course that every product has to be correctly marketed before it will realise that value). I would say that the bare minimum is a mid-price synth, a reverb unit (if the synth doesn't have it built in) and an inexpensive portable DAT recorder such as the Casio DA-7. This little lot could cost under £1000 if you shopped carefully and scanned the small ads. You would be limited to very simple types of music unless you added more equipment, but even simple pieces can sell very well indeed and you will hear plenty in the soundtracks of TV programmes and on the radio. I have had dozens of tracks published that I did on a budget eight track in the days when budget eight tracks weren't anything to rave about. Between selling my 8-track and waiting for my 16-track to be delivered I used a simple Fostex cassette multitracker in conjunction with an Akai sampler and a sequencer to produce twenty or so tracks that have since appeared on CD. The basic rule is to work within the limitations of your equipment, exploit its strengths and conceal its weaknesses.

Can I master onto cassette?

For your own use and demos, the final stereo master can be a cassette. But the quality of even the best cassettes just doesn't compare to a DAT or half decent reel-to-reel. Get your practice in with a cassette deck, and then when you think you are up to it – invest. You certainly won't regret it and you'll be able to produce a master recording that is acceptable by publishers, record companies and record and CD manufacturers.

How long does it take to record the average song?

The clever answer is that if you are only recording average songs, then then I don't know why you're bothering! It takes as long as it takes basically. I heard a radio interview with a recording artist of moderate stature who was saying how he and his band recorded two hundred takes of one song to get it to its finished state. It wasn't much to write home about either, but it does demonstrate that you really have to put everything you've got into your recordings. Other people are, and you'll have to do the same to compete. It wouldn't be anything extraordinary to spend four or five days on one song if you're starting the production process from scratch.

If I can only afford one microphone for my recordings, which one should I buy?

You have to have good equipment, good speakers and good acoustics before microphones get really exciting. After all, they don't have any knobs on them, do they? But professional engineers will talk about the characteristics of microphones all day if you let them, so they must be rather important. Every microphone has its own characteristics and suits some situations more than others. It follows from this that there is no one mic that is suitable for everything. But there are certain models that can almost do no wrong, with the emphasis on the 'almost', one of these being the Neumann U87 which must be just about the classic mic of all time. It's expensive of course, over a grand now, new. But secondhand U87s sometimes become available for less and they can be used on anything from tin whistles to floor toms, although they are usually considered to be at their best for vocals and orchestral section miking. The one thing they are not so good for is co-incident stereo miking, not in my opinion anyway.

At the cheaper end of the spectrum the Shure SM58 is a good vocal mic, and can probably be regarded as the lowest cost fully pro mic. The only snag is that it doesn't have a wonderful top end response so it's virtually useless for metallic percussion – tambourines etc. As a relatively inexpensive all-rounder, I can recommend the Beyer Dynamic M201 which will handle just about everything with a high degree of competence.

I have some MIDI equipment but no recording gear. Should I expand my MIDI system or buy a multitrack?

You have to buy a multitrack! The best part of using a MIDI system is when you have worked up the composition to a reasonable state and then start laying it down onto the multitrack tape. As it builds up track by track the whole thing really comes alive. I don't know why this is so, but it's like the difference between sitting in a hot stuffy room, and then opening the windows and letting in a breath of fresh air. And once the transfer is done, your MIDI system is freed up to add a whole new kaleidoscope of creativity.

I can only afford one 8-track digital multitrack. Can I make serious recordings?

Once upon a time you would have had to sell your 8-track machine to buy a 16-track or 24-track recorder. Now you can simply add another machine and they will synchronise together very easily. Eight tracks did seem to be enough for the Beatles, in their later years, and the early Pink Floyd, which demonstrates how much can be achieved with so little, but musical arrangements now tend to be much more complex and you will eventually need those extra tracks. In the meantime, you can achieve a lot on eight tracks by using the bouncing techniques outlined in Chapter 6. Remember that recording is all about making music and it's not necessarily about demonstrating how much equipment you have at your disposal. I've made CDs on 8-track and I don't see why anyone else can't.

Should I add EQ and effects while I'm multitracking, or leave them until the mix?

Leaving effects and EQ until the mix is 'playing safe'. There are indeed times when it's best to play safe, and other times when there may be more reward for living dangerously. If you have invited a vocalist or instrumentalist into your studio and negotiated a special rate (tea and biscuits?), then it makes a lot of sense to play safe. Get the cleanest, most accurate recording you can and take pains to make sure that there are no faults such as misreadings in the lyrics, wrong notes etc.

Then when the musician has gone home and you are left alone in your laboratory you can carry out all the fiendish experiments your imagination can devise, safe in the knowledge that you can start back from square one at any time you like.

But, at the other extreme, if you have a controlled source such as a synth or sampler playing under the direction of a sequencer, then it would be a criminal waste of an opportunity not to have a go at doing something to the sound as you record it to multitrack, otherwise you are playing parrot to the factory programmer's "Who's a pretty boy then?".

What you do to the track is up to you, whether it's EQ or a little bit of 'room' sound, but of course you must bear in mind that the track will have to harmonise with the rest of the mix. The great thing is that if at any later stage you don't like what you have done, the raw track can be repeated at the push of a couple of buttons. Adding a little extra creativity to the basic sounds you use is adding value to the mix and making your recording more personal.

Why can't I get a great drum sound like I hear on record or CD?
Let's redefine the question to 'sampled drum sound' since recording real drums well is a specialist art form in its own right, and you wouldn't really expect to compete with first rate studios and engineers in your bedroom. But it should in theory be a piece of cake to match the quality of sampled drum tracks since the quality of the drums (assuming you are using good source material) is there already. But the old saying, it's not what you have it's what you do with it, finds its true meaning in this situation.

It's a rare studio recording where the drums have not undergone processing of some kind, even if the sounds were basically good to start with. Big mixers have sophisticated EQ, and a good monitoring environment helps enormously in getting a good drum sound because you can fine tune each component with almost limitless precision. You can't do that at home because you can't hear the sound as clearly and accurately, and you probably don't have quite as full a selection of tools.

This may sound slightly negative, but one has to do the best one can and work within the limitation that if you want the drum sound to form the basis of your production technique then you're going to have to work hard. But there is an alternative. It is becoming a rather more accepted practice than it used to be to sample drum beats from commercial recordings and loop them to back your own music, although it still isn't legal. This way you get a 'studio produced' drum track, and you add the instruments on top. Of course this risks compromising your creativity and you have to ask yourself, is the music still yours?

Also, if you plan on having the recording released, then the owner of the recording you sampled has a right to prevent you doing so (in fact he had a right in theory to stop you sampling the drum beat in the first place). In practice, these difficulties can be overcome if the end result is good enough. The moral is, if you can't solve a problem by tackling it head on, try and sidestep it. There's always another way.

My mix sounds great in the studio but not so good elsewhere. What can I do?

This is a classic situation. Something similar occurs when a mix sounds good played loud, but loses an inordinate amount of impact played at a normal level. It's very easy to get carried away by the overall sound of a mix and not listen to it sufficiently analytically. The relevant strengths of the important structural instruments have to be judged very carefully, particularly the balance of the bass drum and bass synth or guitar between themselves and with the rest of the mix.

Also, the ear (or more accurately, the brain) has a system for ignoring prominent sounds which go on too long, so that synth line which sounds just right when you let the mix wash over you may in fact be too loud, and it may jump out of the speakers and poke you in the ear when you listen the next day.

As I have said earlier, it's vital to try out your mix on different systems before you draw a line under it and call it finished (a work of art is never finished, so they say, only abandoned). Try it out at low level too. It's often instructive to turn the mix right down until most of the instruments are inaudible. You may find that one is more prominent than you expected and it may need to be dealt with by pulling down the fader or providing some EQ cut in its predominant frequency band. If you have really big speakers you may find yourself tempted to put a very deep bass or bass drum on the recording.

Watch out then that it doesn't disappear completely when played on small domestic speakers because it is below their frequency range. If your monitors have a particularly 'tight' bass end, then it's also tempting to load on the LF, and then you find that the cones of ordinary speakers flap around uncontrollably because you're asking them to handle more bass than they really can.

The vocalist I'm using sounds great on stage but terrible in the studio. What can I do?

Another common complaint. It's true that poor intonation can go unnoticed in the excitement of a live gig, but it shows up only too strongly in the studio. It is very difficult to judge pitch when you're listening on headphones and it's an exceptional vocalist who has such a good innate sense of pitch that he or she can produce the right note without being able to hear what's going on properly. A partial solution is to slip one headphone slightly behind the ear so that some sound can enter naturally.

A better, but more complex, solution is to let the vocalist monitor on loudspeakers. Of course, a certain amount of crosstalk will be recorded along with the vocal, but much of it can be eliminated by recording, on another track, just the crosstalk through the mic, but with the phase button pressed. When you add this to the vocal track a lot of the crosstalk will be cancelled. If you do this, bear in mind that the mic has to stay in exactly the same position. It's not something you can come back and do a couple of days later.

If a vocalist has something less than a full, impressive vocal timbre, he or she can be thickened up by the traditional technique of double tracking. No, you don't need an expensive effects unit to do this, just a spare track on the tape and a lot of patience. The vocalist simply repeats his or her part exactly and it results in a very professional sound nearly always. In fact, this technique works so well that effects units can't even begin to approach the quality that can be achieved. Problems crop up when there are slight discrepancies in the timing of consonants and the length of words.

The way to deal with the consonant problem is simply to miss out the troublesome ones on the second track. For example if a line ends with the word 'feet' (no-one's going to sue me for copyright on that example), then on the second pass the vocalist should just sing 'fee' and no-one will know the difference. Getting the length of all the words right is a matter of trial, error, practice and patience.

My recordings are basically good, but how can I give them some extra 'professional' polish?

As you may have gathered, I'm a great believer in the power of EQ and hope that manufacturers will one day give us the power of expensive units at a more reasonable cost. After your mix is finished and is as good as you can get it with your existing equipment it may be worthwhile hiring some extra gear to take it just one stage further. It's common practice to EQ the final stereo mix before it's transferred to record or CD, sometimes to iron out problems, sometimes to add a little more 'magic'. If you can get hold of a good equaliser and a second stereo machine then you can do this before the mix leaves your studio.

One way to do it is to get out a CD which you think sounds great and play it over your monitors for 15 minutes or so. Then change over to your track and start equalising, not to copy the sound of the

CD but just so that you like what you hear, your ears already attuned to a sound you like. Work at this for a maximum of half an hour so your ears don't get tired, then have a long break. Come back from the break suitably refreshed and play the track without EQ, then play it with the EQ. If it's better then make a recording, take note of the make and model of the EQ unit and the settings you used and be sure to label the original master and your new version carefully.

Compression can also be used on a mix, although it's not as universally applicable. If you can hire a unit which has the so-called 'soft-knee' feature then so much the better. Experiment with EQ and compression and see what you can achieve.

My recordings are, frankly, boring. I've heard much more interesting recordings that use far fewer instruments. Where am I going wrong?

You are not going wrong, you are going right – because you're at the stage where you have developed a real appreciation of the recording engineer's art. The next stage is to be able to achieve similar results yourself.

One prime cause of uninteresting, 'sterile', recordings is an excess of precision and exactitude. There comes a point when you go beyond getting things right and start to sound like a machine. And come to think of it, with so many machines in our studios anyway, how can we stop music becoming mechanical? It boils down to artistic judgment. This is something that needs to be liberally applied at every stage of the recording process. It's very easy to record a pattern into a sequencer and then press the quantise button automatically, without thinking. But it's much better to listen first and ask yourself whether the track or pattern needs to be quantised. If it does, then quantise it, but keep the original version just in case.

Sometimes there may be just the odd note seriously out of place, in which case simply edit that one note. It can be a difficult thing to do, to judge when something is 'perfect enough' and not over perfect. And when you are judging against sequencer-style precision it's difficult not to think that your playing is inaccurate. But small inaccuracies give music life and vigour, and that needs to be preserved as much as possible.

Another cause of boredom in a mix is the repetition of sounds. If you use a sampler, then you may have the same snare drum beat occurring well over a hundred times in a song. Find ways of varying repetitive tracks. Instead of just using the same snare all the way through, how about making a group of three notes with the two outer ones tuned respectively slightly – and almost inaudibly – up and down. If you use these at random points, it will go some way toward the situation where a real drummer, no matter how skilled, can never make two snare drum hits exactly the same. Finding ways of adding variations in timing and timbre will add life to your mix.

How can I make my recordings different to everyone else's?

Simple – go easy on the factory programs in your synth. They may sound great, but everyone else is using them too. Shortly after acquiring a multi-effects unit I spent an enjoyable half an hour erasing all the factory programs (actually it wasn't enjoyable because I had to unlock all the presets before I could overwrite them). I knew that I would be losing some good'uns, but I hope to make more of my own, and what's more I have made a conscious decision not to re-use effects but to create them from scratch each time.

It's going to take a little longer but I want to make music, not run a production line. The moral is to take your inspiration from other people, but use every opportunity you have to make your sound your own, by creating sounds from raw materials or by combining existing sounds in new ways.

I want to be a pro engineer. What do I do?

I have to ask a personal question here: How old are you? If you are under 23 then you can choose Route 1, if your teeth are rather longer and your hair a bit greyer then you'll have to go via Route 2. There are now a lot of recording studios about, there are over two hundred commercial studios in London alone and many more dotted around the country. These studios all need staffing and from time to time a job vacancy will crop up. The best chance you'll get of snapping up such a vacancy is by knowing someone who's in the know – recording engineering isn't the type of job where you can get in on a couple of exam passes.

Route 1 is into a commercial studio and you have to be young, sixteen to eighteen being the optimum age. You can start by writing to all the studios you can find (in the Yellow Pages and elsewhere) and showing an interest by asking if you can pay them a visit because you are keen to get into recording. Note that you haven't actually asked for a job, studios get so many letters from people wanting employment that they often get filed under 'B' (for bin). But if you can wangle your way in and impress the manager, then there's always the chance that he'll remember you when a vacancy does occur. Another way of getting to meet the right people is to sign on with a studio engineering course.

If you are between 16 and 18, ask your careers advisor about

Further Education courses in sound engineering, and don't accept 'there's no such thing' for an answer because it's not true. If you get on a course like this you could be placed in a studio for four days a week and spend the other day at college. How much of a success you make of this is purely up to you, you have to impress the studio that you're worth employing when your training period ends.

Route 2 is for when you have passed your studio sell by date. The most realistic thing to do is set up your own studio, preferably in partnership with someone who understands the business well. An alternative is to look for work in a related field such as PA or Audio Visual where they are not quite so age conscious (but try to be under 30!) about prospective new employees. Don't imagine that you are too old for education either. Both private and publicly funded colleges will, almost certainly, judge you on your enthusiasm and commitment. They usually don't accept everybody who applies, but if you have read this book you are off to a good start!

However you get into recording, if you are going to take it more seriously than a hobby, be prepared for a lot of hard work and long hours. Come to think of it, you can spend a lot of time tinkering around in the spare room studio just for the fun of it. Recording engineering is a particularly rewarding thing to do, because for every little bit of extra effort you put in, there is that little bit of extra return in the form of a better recording.

Perhaps your ambitions go no further than harmless enjoyment out of the public gaze, or maybe you want to see yourself behind a mighty SSL console in a few years time. Wherever your recording takes you, I hope this book will have helped just a little and I wish you good luck with whatever you do.

Recording studios in the UK

Abbey Road Studios, 3 Abbey Road,
London, NW8 9AY
Tel: 0171 266 7000
Fax: 0171 266 7250

Air Edel Studios, 18 Rodmarton
Street, London, W1H 3FW
Tel: 0171 486 6466
Fax: 0171 224 0344

Air Studios, Lyndhurst Hall,
Lyndhurst Road, Hampstead,
London, NW3 5NG
Tel: 0171 794 0660
Fax: 0171 794 8518

Battery Studios,1 Maybury Gardens,
London, NW10 2SG
Tel: 0181 459 8899
Fax: 0181 459 8 732

Beethoven Street Studios, 56
Beethoven Street, London, W10 4LG
Tel: 0181 960 1088
Fax: 0181 969 5231

BJG Recording Unit,18 A/B, 101
Farm Lane, London, SW6 1QL
Tel: 0171 381 6298
Fax: 0171 385 6105

The Church Studios, 145H Crouch
Hill, London, N8 9QH
Tel: 0181 340 9779
Fax: 0181 348 3346

CTS Studios, Engineers Way,
Wembley, Middx, HA9 0DR
Tel: 0181 903 4611
Fax: 0181 903 7130

Decca Record Company Ltd, 254/6
Belsize Road, London, NW6 4BT
Tel: 0181 742 5595
Fax: 0181 742 5596

Eden Studios, 20-24 Beaumont
Road, London, W4 5AP
Tel: 0181 995 5432
Fax: 0181 747 1931

The Exchange, 42 Bruges Place,
Randolph Street, London, NW1 OTX
Tel: 0171 485 0530
Fax: 0171 482 4588

Finesplice Ltd, 1 Summer House
Lane, Harmondsworth, West
Drayton, Middx UB7 0AW
Tel: 0181 564 78 39
Fax: 0181 759 9629

Gateway Studio, Kingston Hill
Centre, Kingston-Upon-Thames,
Surrey, KT2 7LB
Tel: 0181 549 0014
Fax: 0181 547 7337

ICC Studios, 4 Regency Mews,
Silverdale Road, Eastbourne, Sussex
BN20 7AB
Tel: 01323 643341
Fax: 01323 649240

Jacobs Studio Ltd, Ridgway House,
Runwick Lane, Nr Farnham, Surrey
GU10 5EE
Tel: 01252 715546
Fax: 01252 712846

Konk Recording Studio, 84-86
Tottenham Lane, London, N8 7EE
Tel: 0181 340 7873
Fax: 0181 348 3952

Lansdowne Recording Studio,
Lansdowne House, Lansdowne Road,
London,W11 3LP
Tel: 0171 727 0041
Fax: 0171 792 8904

Logorhythm, 6-10 Lexington Street,
London, W1R 3HS
Tel: 0171 734 7443
Fax: 0171 439 7057

M2 Facilities Group, The Forum, 74-
80 Camden Street, London, NW1
OEG
Tel: 0171 387 5001
Fax: 0171 387 5025

Manor Mobiles, The Manor, Skipton-
on-Cherwell, Near Kidlington, Oxon,
OX5 1OL
Tel: 018653 77552
Fax: 018653 77116

Marcus Recording Studios, 17-21
Wyfold Road, Fulham, London, SW6
6SE
Tel: 0171 385 3366
Fax: 0171 381 2680

Metropolis, The Powerhouse, 70
Chiswick High Road, London, W4
1SY
Tel: 0181 742 1111
Fax: 0181 742 2626

Milo Music Ltd, 43-44 Hoxton
Square, London, N1 6PB
Tel: 0171 729 4100
Fax: 0171 729 7400

Modus Music, The Old Rectory,
Church Lane, Exning, Nr Newmarket,
Suffolk CB8 7HT
Tel: 01638 577324
Fax: 01638 577106

Molinare, 34 Fouberts Place,
London, W1V 2BH
Tel: 0171 439 2244
Fax: 0171 734 6813

Network Music and Media, Network House, 22A Forest Road West, Nottingham NG7 4EQ
Tel: 0115 9784714
Fax: 0115 9424183

Olympic Studios, 117 Church Road, Barnes, London, SW13 9HL
Tel: 0181 748 7961
Fax: 0181 748 3067

Orinoco, 36 Leroy Street, London, SE1 4SS
Tel: 0171 232 0008
Fax: 0171 237 6109

Polygram Record Operations UK, 1 Sussex Place, Hammersmith, London, W6 9XS
Tel: 0181 846 8515 }
Fax: 0181 741 4901

R G Jones Studios, Beulah Road, Wimbledon, London, SW19 3SB
Tel: 0181 540 9881
Fax: 0181 542 4368

RAK Recording Studios, 42-48 Charlbert Street, London, NW8 7BU
Tel: 0171 586 2012
Fax: 0171 722 5823

Rewind Studios, The Media Centre, 131-151 Great Titchfield Street, London W1P 8AE
Tel: 0171 577 7774
Fax: 0171 577 7771

Ridge Farm Studios, Rusper Road, Capel, Dorking, Surrey RH5 5HG
Tel: 01306 711202
Fax: 01306 711626

RNIB Talking Book Service, 206 Great Portland Street, London, W1
Tel: 0171 388 1266
Fax: 0171 383 7288

Rockfield Studios, Amberley Court, Monmouth, South Wales, NP5 4ET
Tel: 01600 712449
Fax: 01600 714421

Sain (Recordiau) Cyf, Llandwrog, Caernarfon, Gwynedd, Wales, LL54 5TG
Tel: 01286 831111
Fax: 01286 831497

Sarm East, 9 - 13 Osborn Street, London, E1 6TD
Tel: 0171 247 1311
Fax: 0171 221 9247

Sarm Hook End, Hook End Manor, Checkendon, Nr Reading, Berks RG8 0UE
Tel: 01491 681000
Fax: 01491 681926

Sarm West, 8-10 Basing Street, London, W11 1ET
Tel: 0171 229 1229
Fax: 0171 221 9247

Sawmills Studio, Golant, Fowey, Cornwall, PL23 1LP
Tel: 01726 833338
Fax: 01726 832015

Scottys Sound Studio, 17-22 Newtown Street, Kilsyth, Glasgow, G65 0JX
Tel: 01236 825843
Fax: 01236 825683

Select Sound Studio, Big M House, 1 Stevenage Road, Knebworth, Herts SG3 6AN
Tel: 01438 814433
Fax: 01438 815252

Snake Ranch Studio, 90 Lots Road, London, SW10 0QD
Tel: 0171 351 7888
Fax: 0171 352 5194

Soho Square Recording Studios, 22 Soho Square, London W1V 5FJ
Tel: 0171 734 6670
Fax: 0171 734 6675

SRT Mastering, Edison Road, St Ives, Cambs, PE17 4LF
Tel: 01480 461880
Fax: 01480 496100

Stiwdio Sain, Canolfan Sain, Llandwrog, Caernarfon, Gwynedd LL54 5TG}
Tel: 01286 831111
Fax: 01286 831497

Strongroom Ltd, The Bank, 120 Curtain Road, London, EC2A 3PJ
Tel: 0171 729 6165
Fax: 0171 729 6218

Swanyard Studios, 12-27 Swan Yard, Islington, London, N1 1SD
Tel: 0171 354 3737
Fax: 0171 226 2581

The Town House, 150 Goldhawk Road, Shepherds Bush, London, W12 8HH
Tel: 0181 932 3200
Fax: 0181 932 3207

Videosonics, 13 Hawley Crescent, London, NW1 8NP
Tel: 0171 209 0209
Fax: 0171 419 4460

West Side Studios, Olaf Centre, 10 Olaf Street, London, W11 4BE
Tel: 0171 221 9494
Fax: 0171 727 0008

Whitfield Street Recording Studios, 31-37 Whitfield Street, London, W1P 5RE
Tel: 0171 636 3434
Fax: 0171 323 5964

The Windings, Ffrwd Valley, Wrexham, Clwyd, LL12 9TH
Tel: 01978 720420
Fax: 01978 720503

Wool Hall Studios, Castle Corner, Beckington Nr Bath, Somerset, BA3 6TA
Tel: 01373 830731
Fax: 01373 830679

The Workhouse, 488 Old Kent Road, London, SE1 5AG
Tel: 0171 237 1737
Fax: 0171 231 7658

There are many other studios besides those listed here. Look in your local Yellow Pages and the Yellow Pages directories of other areas, which are often available in public libraries. Look in the classified advertisements in music and recording magazines and weeklies. Search the Internet for 'recording studio'. If all else fails think of a clever name and buy a Portastudio!

19 | Glossary of terms

Acoustics

More properly called 'room acoustics'. The interaction between sound and the surfaces in a room or auditorium.

Acoustic treatment

Measures taken to improve the subjective sound quality of a room.

Adaptor

A short cable or connector which allows two normally incompatible connectors to be mated.

ADAT

Proprietary digital multitrack recording format of Alesis.

Auxiliary return

A mixing console input similar to a channel but with reduced facilities, usually just level and pan. Often used for reverb and other effects units.

Auxiliary send

Besides the normal group outputs routed to the multitrack tape recorder, mixing consoles have auxiliary sends to route signal to fold-back and effects units.

Balanced connection

A method of connection which uses two signal conductors plus a screen to cancel out interference picked up in the cable. Usually only professional equipment is balanced. Semi-professional and domestic equipment is unbalanced.

Bantam jack

A small version of the GPO jack connector. Used in patchbays.

BNC

A type of video connector.

Capacitance

Electrical phenomenon where a high frequency signal passes between two conductors even when there is no direct connection.

Capacitor microphone

A high quality microphone which exploits the capacitance effect and needs to be powered.

Cassette recorder

Domestic cassette, not to be confused with a reel-to-reel tape recorder.

Channel

One input section of a mixing console. Typical consoles suitable for the small studio have 16 to 24 channels.

Chinagraph

Wax pencil used for marking tape for editing.

Commercial studio

A studio available for hire.

Compressor

Device used to reduce the difference between high and low level signals.

DAT

Digital audio tape. Originally proposed as a replacement for the domestic cassette but suitable for professional quality stereo recording.

DCC

Digital compact cassette. A proposed replacement for the traditional cassette, acceptable for mastering but not quite as suitable as DAT.

Decibel

Used to compare the level of sound signals, whether real sounds travelling in air, electrical signals in a mixing console or magnetic recordings.

Demo

A recording made to play to a publisher or record company, not for commercial release.

Digital delay

Device used to produce single and multiple echoes.

Disk recorder

A digital recorder which uses a computer hard disk or optical disk instead of tape. Sometimes called a hard disk recorder.

DTRS

Digital 8-track multitrack recording format invented by Tascam.

Dynamic microphone

A type of microphone which does not need powering, but typically does not sound as good as a capacitor microphone.

Dynamic range

The difference in level between the loudest and the quietest sections of a recording.

Earth loop

When there is more than one connection to mains earth in a system, a low pitched hum will be heard through the speakers.

Earth

The planet we live on. Electrical systems use the Earth as a zero voltage reference and a sink for unwanted currents.

Editing block

Metal block used to align tape ready for joining.

Effects

Devices connected to the mixing console to enhance a sound.

Electronic balancing

System of making a balanced connection in equipment which does not use transformers.

EQ

Equalisation. Each channel of the mixing console will have an EQ section which is used to balance the levels of high, middle and low frequencies.

Expander

A rack mounting unit which has the sound producing capabilities of a synthesiser or sampler, but is driven by MIDI rather than a keyboard.

Foldback

Headphone monitoring for musicians in the studio.

Faders

Controls on the mixing console to balance the levels of a number of signals.

FX

Abbreviation for 'effects'.

Gain

Control on the mixing console designed to adjust the level of an incoming signal to a level suitable for the console.

Gaffer tape

Strong cloth sticky tape often used by sound engineers.

GPO jack connector

Type of connector used in patchbays.

Half track stereo

A stereo reel-to-reel tape recorder which records two channels of audio across practically the full width of the tape.

Home studio

Studio set up for the benefit of an individual. Not normally available for hire.

Hum

Low pitched buzz. A common form of electrical interference usually caused by an earth loop.

IEC

A European body which sets standards on various things such as tape recorder equalisation and mains connectors.

Interference

Unwanted electrical signals contaminating the sound signal.

IPS

Abbreviation for inches per second.

Isopropyl alcohol

Type of alcohol used for cleaning tape heads.

Jackfield

English version of the American term 'patchbay'.

Jack connector

Cylindrical connector often used by musicians, also finding a use in the semi-professional studio.

Level

The loudness of an acoustic or electrical signal.

Loom

A number of individual cables gathered together.

Master

1) The stereo tape recorder.
2) The output section of a mixing console which is connected to the stereo tape recorder.
3) The finished recording.

MIDI

Musical instrument digital interface. Used for connecting synthesisers, samplers, expanders and keyboards etc together.

MIDI time code (MTC)

A timing signal sent down a MIDI cable to allow synchronisation between MIDI devices.

Mixing console

The nerve centre of the recording studio where all the signals come together and are blended to taste.

Module

Another name for 'Expander'.

Monitor

1) Short for 'monitor loudspeaker'.

2) To listen closely to the loudspeakers.

3) Controls on the mixing console used for listening to the output of the multitrack tape recorder while overdubbing.

Multi-effects unit

Device capable of several different types of effect.

Multicore cable

Cable which carries several separate audio signals.

Multitrack

Short for 'multitrack tape recorder'. A tape recorder which can record several different musical lines on different tracks spaced across the width of the tape.

NAB spool

$10^{1}/_{2}$ inch spool with a large centre hole.

NAB

An American body which sets standards on various things such as tape recorder equalisation and tape spools.

Near field monitors

Small loudspeakers mounted close to the engineer's listening position.

Noise gate

Device used for cutting out background noise when an instrument is not playing.

Normalling

Patchbay wiring technique which reduces the need for patchcords in a normal recording situation.

Outboard

Effects units.

Pan

A mixing console control which changes the apparent position of a signal between the stereo speakers.

Parallel

Term used when one output is connected to two or more inputs.

Patchbay

A unit with many GPO jack sockets which are connected to virtually all the inputs and outputs of the equipment in the studio. Saves searching round the back of the equipment for the connectors.

Patchcords

Short cables used for connecting equipment via the patchbay.

PA

Abbreviation for 'public address'.

Phono connector

Potentially unreliable hifi connector pressed into service in some equipment designed for the small studio.

Plasterboard

Material commonly used for sound insulation.

Portastudio

A multitrack cassette recorder with integral mixer. A trade name of Tascam.

Power amplifier

An amplifier without controls, other than level, that drives the monitor speakers.

Producer

The person who is responsible for the musical qualities of the recording.

Quarter track stereo

A system of stereo tape recording which records two tracks on HALF the width of the tape. Totally unsuitable for the recording studio.

Recording engineer

The person who operates the mixing console and recording equipment in the studio.

Rack

Virtually all studio equipment, unless it is designed to be free standing, has standard fixings for mounting in a 19" rack.

Reel-to-reel

Tape recorder suitable for studio use. Not to be confused with the domestic cassette recorder.

Reverb

Device which simulates the natural echoes in a room.

Sampler

Device which can record sound digitally and play it back at different pitches, controlled by a MIDI keyboard.

Sequencer

Device for recording and manipulating MIDI data, such as that produced by a MIDI keyboard. May be a dedicated unit but is often supplied as computer software.

SMPTE

An American body, known particularly for its timecode standards.

Splicing tape

Special sticky tape used for joining recording tape in editing.

Synchronisation

Linking together a MIDI sequencer and tape recorder, tape and video, or two or more tape recorders.

Synthesiser

Musical instrument which generates sound from electronic or digital circuits.

Timecode

An audio signal used to synchronise recorders, sequencers and console automation systems.

Track

On a tape recorder, each track carries a separate musical line.

Type A jack

The standard $^1/_4$ inch jack connector.

Type B jack

The GPO jack connector.

U

The unit of vertical 19 inch rack space. 1U = $1^3/_4$ inches.

XLR connector

The standard professional audio connector.

Index

How to set up a
Home Recording Studio

David Mellor

108 pp • 244 x 172 mm • illustrated
ISBN 1 870775 43 0

★ Updated and expanded edition
★ New section on MIDI in the studio
★ Covers project studios and DJ studios
★ New sections on acoustics and soundproofing
★ Details on equipment, wiring and patchbays
★ For musicians, recording enthusiasts and DJs
★ Glossary of terms; lists of useful addresses

£10.95
inc P&P

If you're thinking of setting up a home studio. a project studio or a DJ studio, this book is the place to start. It takes a highly practical 'nuts and bolts' type of approach to help you produce an efficient and productive studio.

It covers soundproofing – keeping the sound in and the noise out – acoustics, studio layout, and studio equipment – with advice on the kit you are likely to need. There's a chapter on studio furniture, and the practical theme is continued with sections on cabling, wiring looms and even soldering, all highly illustrated.

A section is devoted to the layout and wiring of the patchbay, and the book ends with an invaluable questions and answers section, a glossary of terms and a list of contacts.

Contents: Types of home studio. Soundproofing. Acoustics and layout. Studio furniture and decor. Cables. Soldering techniques and wiring looms. Patcbays. Bits and pieces. Questions and answers. Glossary. Directory of manufacturers and suppliers.

Call our order hotline 01732 770893

PC Publishing

Tel 01732 770893 • Fax 01732 770268
email pcp@cix.compulink.co.uk • website http://www.pc-pubs.demon.co.uk